Best Air Fryer Cookbook for Beginners

Easy and Healthy Air Fryer Recipes for Any Taste

By

Henry Wilson

Copyright [Henry Wilson]

All rights reserved. No part of this guide may be reproduced in any form without permission in writing from the publisher except in the case of brief quotations embodied in critical articles or reviews.

Legal & Disclaimer

The information contained in this book and its contents is not designed to replace or take the place of any form of medical or professional advice; and is not meant to replace the need for independent medical, financial, legal, or other professional advice or services, as may be required. The content and information in this book have been provided for educational and entertainment purposes only.

The content and information contained in this book have been compiled from sources deemed reliable, and it is accurate to the best of the Author's knowledge, information, and belief. However, the Author cannot guarantee its accuracy and validity and cannot be held liable for any errors and/or omissions. Further, changes are periodically made to this book as and when needed. Where appropriate and/or necessary, you must consult a professional (including but not limited to your doctor, attorney, financial advisor or such other professional advisor) before using any of the suggested remedies, techniques, or information in this book.

Upon using the contents and information contained in this book, you agree to hold harmless the Author from and against any damages, costs, and expenses, including any legal fees potentially resulting from the application of any of the information provided by this book. This disclaimer applies to any of the loss, damages or injury caused by the use and application, whether directly or indirectly, of any advice or information presented, whether for breach of contract, tort, negligence, personal injury, criminal intent, or under any other cause of action.

You agree to accept all risks of using the information presented in this book.

You agree that, by continuing to read this book, where appropriate and/or necessary, you shall consult a professional (including but not limited to your doctor, attorney, or financial advisor or such other advisor as needed) before using any of the suggested remedies, techniques, or information in this book.

TABLE OF CONTENTS

Introduction 1
INTRODUCTION TO AIR FRYERS 2
THE BENEFITS OF AN AIR FRYER 3
The Function of an Air Fryer 4
1. Breakfasts.. 6
   Air Fryer Baked Apples... 6
   Air Fryer French Toast 8
   Air Fryer Frittata..10
   Air Fryer Puffed Egg Tarts 12
   Air Fryer Hash Browns 14
   Air Fryer Bacon...16
   Air Fryer Omelette 18
   Air Fryer Breakfast Pockets 20
   Flourless Broccoli Quiche...................................... 22
   Breakfast Style Air Fryer Potatoes......................... 24
2. Lunches 26
   Healthy Fish Finger Sandwich 26
   Chicken Quesadillas.. 29
   6 Minute Pita Bread Cheese Pizza 31
   Simple Cheese Sandwich 33
   Air Fryer Hot Dogs..35
   Bourbon Bacon Burger 37

 Leftover Turkey & Cheese Calzone 40

 Air Fryer Chick-fil-A Nuggets 43

 Air Fried Chicken Tenders 45

 Roast Chicken 47

3. Appetizers and Sides 49

 Beetroot Chips 49

 Air-Fried Shishito Peppers 52

 Air-Fryer French Fries 54

 Coconut Shrimp With Spicy Marmalade Sauce 56

 Air Fryer Baked Sweet Potato 58

 Jalapeño Poppers 60

 Pork Taquitos 62

 Taco Bell Crunch Wraps 64

 Panko Breaded Chicken Parmesan With Marinara Sauce 66

 Apple Cinnamon Dessert Empanadas 68

4. Fish and Seafoods 70

 3 Ingredient Fried Catfish 70

 Crumbed Fish 72

 Cajun Salmon 74

 Crunchy Air Fryer Sushi Roll 76

 BANG BANG Fried Shrimp 79

 Airfried Salmon Patties 81

 Honey-Glazed Salmon 84

 Cajun Shrimp 86

 Spicy Fish Street Tacos with Sriracha Slaw 88

 Zesty Ranch Air Fryer Fish Fillets 91

5. Poultry Recipes 93

Chicken Parmesan 93
Air Fryer Sriracha-Honey Chicken Wings.................................95
Tandoori Chicken 97
Zinger Chicken Burger... 100
Garlic Parmesan Chicken Wings 102
Air Fryer Rotisserie Chicken 104
Air-Fryer Garlic Parmesan Chicken Tenders 106
Air Fryer Pizza Stuffed Chicken...108
Air-Fryer Thai Peanut Chicken Egg Rolls 110
Air Fryer Chicken Nuggets 112
Air Fryer Lemon Pepper Chicken 114
Nashville Hot Chicken 116
Air-Fried Buttermilk Chicken.. 118
Copycat KFC Popcorn Chicken 121
Chicken Tikkas...123
Flourless Chicken Cordon Bleu 126
Air Fryer KFC Chicken Strips 128
Pickle-Brined Fried Chicken..130
Air Fryer Southern-Style Chicken 133
Air Fryer Ranch Chicken Tenders 135

6. Meat Recipes 138
Stromboli 138
Roasted Stuffed Peppers..140
Air Fryer Beef Empanadas...142
Air-Fried Turkey Breast with Maple Mustard Glaze............144
Crispy Boneless Breaded Pork Chops....................................146
Turkey Breast with Cherry Glaze..148

Air Fryer Coffee & Spice Ribeye 150
Air Fried Meatloaf 152
Air Fryer Chinese Salt and Pepper Pork Chops 154
Air Fryer Country Fried Steak... 157
Air Fryer Italian-Style Meatballs 159
Air Fried Pork Chops With Brussels Sprouts 161
Thanksgiving Turkey... 163
Ultimate Air Fryer Burgers 165
Perfect Air Fryer Steak with Garlic Herb Butter........................ 167
Air Fryer Mongolian Beef.. 169
Air Fryer Beef Stir Fry With Homemade Marinade 171
Air Fryer Marinated Steak 173
Air Fryer Paleo Sirloin Steak.. 176
Air Fryer Steak Fajita's... 178

7. Vegetable Recipes 180
Air Fryer Fried Ravioli 180
Spicy Cauliflower Stir-Fry 182
Air Fried Cauliflower Rice... 184
Air Fried Sticky Mushroom Rice.. 187
Air-Fried Asparagus 189
Air Fried Zucchini, Yellow Squash, and Carrots....................... 191
Healthy Mediterranean Vegetables 193
Lemony Green Beans 195
Crispy Roasted Broccoli 197
Roasted Rainbow Vegetables 200

8. Desserts.. 202
Nutella-Banana Sandwiches 202

Molten Lava Cake 204
Shortbread Heart Cookies 206
Vegan Beignets.. 208
Apple Pie 211
Zebra Butter Cake 214
Thai-Style Fried Bananas 216
Air Fryer Cinnamon Rolls...219
Air Fryer Cranberry Pecan Muffins.................................. 222
Air Fryer Homemade Pop Tarts 224

Conclusion 227

Introduction

In this book, you will find all the information that you will need to make the most of your Air Fryer. There are also 100 recipes given in this book that will help you to cook healthy and tasty food that you can prepare quickly.

The recipes that have been included in this book can be cooked in an Air Fryer. The recipes have also been segregated into different categories for the convenience of the reader. These tried and tested recipes will help you in whipping up a feast by simply making use of one appliance, the Air Fryer.

Air Fryers don't have to be used simply for cooking fries. You can cook so much more than just that. Different breakfast, lunch and dinner recipes have been provided that make use of poultry, meat, seafood and vegetables for cooking some delicious meals.

INTRODUCTION TO AIR FRYERS

An air fryer is a simple device used to cook foods by making use of hot air. It generates hot air and circulates it around the food, which helps to cook it evenly. This air replaces oils and fats, thereby providing nourishing food that is healthy.

Air fryers have now become quite popular owing to their user friendliness and ease of use. They are now a much sought after modern appliance and one of the most popular kitchen appliances to cook up healthy meals.

The air fryer works on a simple principle known as the Maillard reaction. This reaction helps with crisping up the meal while maintaining the nutritional value, without the use of oils that may be detrimental to health.

THE BENEFITS OF AN AIR FRYER

It replaces other cooking appliances

You can use your air fryer instead of your oven, microwave, deep fryer and dehydrator! In a small device, you can quickly prepare perfect dishes for every meal without sacrificing flavor.

It cooks faster than traditional cooking methods

Air frying works by circulating hot air around the cooking chamber. This results in fast, even cooking, using a fraction of the energy in your oven. Most air fryers can be set to a maximum temperature of 400 ° F. For this reason, just about anything you can do in an oven, you can do in an air fryer.

It uses little or no cooking oil

A main selling point of air fryers is that you can achieve beautifully cooked foods with little to no cooking oil. While that may be attractive to some because it can mean lower fat content, people following the keto diet can rejoice because it means fewer calories, which still matter if you're doing keto for weight loss.

Quick cleaning

Regardless of the cooking method used, your stove may soon become dirty, but with the small cooking chamber and the removable basket of your air fryer, deep cleaning is a breeze!

Henry Wilson

The Function of an Air Fryer

The Air fryer cooks food quite fast owing to this innovative technology and serves up a hearty meal in no time at all. The fryer can be used to cook in many different ways that are outlined as follows:

Roasting foods

Roasting is one of the main ways to cook using an air fryer. The air fryer cuts the time in half when it comes to roasting foods. It makes use of rapid air technology that is designed to cook foods at a faster pace. The advantage is that you spend less time slaving in front of a hot stove and get it done in even less time than you might expect.

Frying foods

The air fryer is also very useful for frying foods. It helps in frying foods at a faster pace without making them too oily. As a matter of fact, you need not worry about using any oil at all, as it effectively fries foods without it. The fryer makes use of hot air alone to crisp up the foods that you want to fry.

Grilling foods

Most of us dread the thought of grilling foods, as we have to prepare the grill for it and get the temperature right to grill the food properly. However, the job becomes much easier with an air fryer. The temperature is preset and all you have to do is place the ingredients in the fryer. Forget about having to flip the food to cook it on both sides, as the fryer will do the job for you.

Baking foods

Just like grilling, the air fryer also bakes foods. Forget having to rely on the traditional oven to bake your foods as the air fryer does the job in half the time. The air fryer gives you almost the same results as a conventional oven and therefore makes for an excellent choice. The air fryer also comes with a baking attachment intended to bake foods. Just like a regular oven, all you have to do is preheat the air fryer and put your food into it.

1. Breakfasts

Air Fryer Baked Apples

Preparation Time: 20 minutes

Yield: 2 Servings

Ingredients

- 1 medium apple or pear
- 2 Tbsp. chopped walnuts

- 2 Tbsp. raisins
- 1 ½ tsp. light margarine, melted
- ¼ tsp. cinnamon
- ¼ tsp. nutmeg
- ¼ cup water

Directions

1. Preheat air fryer to 350° F.
2. Cut the apple or pear in half around the middle and spoon out some of the flesh.
3. Place the apple or pear in frying pan (which may be provided with the air fryer) or on the bottom of the air fryer (after removing the accessory).
4. In a small bowl, combine margarine, cinnamon, nutmeg, walnuts and raisins.
5. Spoon this mixture into the centers of the apple/pear halves.
6. Pour water into the pan.
7. Bake for 20 minutes.

Nutritional Information

- Calories: 194
- Fat: 2g
- Carbs: 23g
- Protein: 4g

Air Fryer French Toast

Preparation Time: 10 minutes

Yield: 2 Servings

Ingredients

- 4 Slices Wholemeal Bread
- 2 Large Eggs
- ¼ Cup Whole Milk
- ¼ Cup Brown Sugar
- 1 Tbsp Honey
- 1 Tsp Cinnamon
- Pinch Of Nutmeg
- Pinch Of Icing Sugar

Directions

1. Chop up your slices of bread into soldiers. Each slice should make 4 soldiers.
2. Place the rest of your ingredients (apart from the icing sugar) into a mixing bowl and mix well.
3. Dip each soldier into the mixture so that it is well coated and then place it into the Air Fryer. When you're done you will have 16 soldiers and then should all be nice and wet from the mixture.
4. Place on 160c for 10 minutes or until they are nice and crispy like toast and are no longer wet. Halfway through cooking turn them over so that both sides of the soldiers have a good chance to be evenly cooked.
5. Serve with a sprinkle of icing sugar and some fresh berries.

Nutritional Information

- Calories: 170
- Fat: 8g
- Carbs: 19g
- Protein: 6g

Air Fryer Frittata

Preparation Time: 20 minutes

Yield: 2 Servings

Ingredients

- 1 cup egg whites
- 2 Tbsp. skim milk
- ¼ cup sliced tomato
- ¼ cup sliced mushrooms
- 2 Tbsp. chopped fresh chives
- Black pepper, to taste

Directions

1. Preheat Air Fryer at 320° F.
2. In a bowl, combine all the ingredients.

3. Transfer to a greased frying pan (which may be provided with the air fryer) or to the bottom of the air fryer (after removing the accessory)
4. Bake for 15 minutes or until frittata is cooked through.

Nutritional Information

1. Calories: 381
2. Fat: 24g
3. Carbs: 2g
4. Protein: 31g

Air Fryer Puffed Egg Tarts

Preparation Time: 20 minutes

Yield: 4 Servings

Ingredients

- 1 cup All-purpose flour
- 1 sheet frozen puff pastry half a 17.3-oz/490 g package, thawed
- 3/4 cup shredded cheese such as Cheddar or Monterey Jack, divided
- 4 large eggs
- 1 tbsp minced fresh parsley or chives optional

Directions

1. On a lightly floured surface, unfold pastry sheet. Cut into 4 squares.
2. Preheat air fryer to 390°F (200°C)
3. Place 2 squares in air fryer basket, spacing them apart. Air-fry for 10 minutes or until pastry is light golden brown.
4. Open basket and, using a metal spoon, press down the centers of each square to make an indentation. Sprinkle 3 tbsp (45 mL) cheese into each indentation and carefully crack an egg into the center of each pastry.
5. Air-fry for 7 to 11 minutes or until eggs are cooked to desired doneness. Transfer to a wire rack set over waxed paper and let cool for 5 minutes. Sprinkle with half the parsley, if desired. Serve warm.
6. Repeat steps 3 to 5 with the remaining pastry squares, cheese, eggs and parsley.

Nutritional Information

- Calories: 446
- Fat: 21g
- Carbs: 27g
- Protein: 14g

Air Fryer Hash Browns

Preparation Time: 20 minutes

Yield: 8 Servings

Ingredients

- Large potatoes - 4 - peeled and finely grated
- Corn flour - 2 tablespoon
- Salt - to taste
- Pepper powder - to taste
- Chili flakes - 2 teaspoon
- Garlic powder - 1 teaspoon (optional)
- Onion Powder - 1 teaspoon (optional)
- Vegetable Oil - 1 + 1 teaspoon

Directions

1. Soak the shredded potatoes in cold water. Drain the water. Repeat the step to drain excess starch from potatoes.
2. In a non-stick pan heat 1 teaspoon of vegetable oil and saute shredded potatoes till cooked slightly for 3-4 mins.
3. Cool it down and transfer the potatoes to a plate.
4. Add corn flour, salt, pepper, garlic and onion powder and chili flakes and mix together roughly.
5. Spread over the plate and pat it firmly with your fingers.
6. Regrigerate it for 20 minutes
7. Preheat air fryer at 180C
8. Take out the now refrigerated potato and divide into equal pieces with a knife
9. Brush the wire basket of the air fryer with little oil
10. Place the hash brown pieces in the basket and fry for 15 minutes at 180C
11. Take out the basket and flip the hash browns at 6 minutes so that they are air fried uniformly
12. Serve it hot with ketchup

Nutritional Information

- Calories: 127
- Fat: 2g
- Carbs: 27g
- Protein: 4g

Air Fryer Bacon

Preparation Time: 10 minutes

Yield: 2 Servings

Ingredients

- 6 strips of bacon
- 2 Slices of Bread

Directions

1. Place the bacon in the bottom of your air fryer basket. I have a 3.5 quart air fryer and was able to get 6 strips of bacon on the bottom. Place the wire rack over your bacon that came with air fryer. This is optional. If you don't have a wire rack that came with your air fryer, then you don't need one.
2. Cook at 350 for 7 to 9 minutes. Open up the air fryer and flip the bacon. Put the air fryer basket back in and cook for another 3 minutes or until however crispy you like your bacon.
3. Put 3 crispy bacon pieces inside 2 bread pieces and enjoy!

Nutritional Information

- Calories: 37
- Fat: 3g
- Carbs: 1g
- Protein: 3g

Air Fryer Omelette

Preparation Time: 10 minutes

Yield: 4 Servings

Ingredients

- 2 eggs
- 1/4 cup milk

- Pinch of salt
- Fresh meat and vegetables, diced (use red bell pepper, green onions, ham and mushrooms)
- 1 teaspoon McCormick Breakfast Seasoning
- 1/4 cup shredded cheese

Directions

1. In a small bowl, mix the eggs and milk until well combined.
2. Add a pinch of salt to the egg mixture.
3. Add your vegetables to the egg mixture.
4. Pour the egg mixture into a well-greased 6"x3" pan.
5. Place the pan into the basket of the air fryer.
6. Cook at 350F Fahrenheit for 8-10 minutes.
7. Halfway through cooking sprinkle the breakfast seasoning onto the eggs and sprinkle the cheese over the top.
8. Use a thin spatula to loosen the omelette from the sides of the pan and transfer to a plate.
9. Garnish with extra green onions, optional

Nutritional Information

- Calories: 274
- Fat: 20g
- Carbs: 6g
- Protein: 13g

Air Fryer Breakfast Pockets

Preparation Time: 10 minutes

Yield: 4 Servings

Ingredients

- one box puff pastry sheets
- 5 eggs
- 1/2 cup sausage crumbled, cooked
- 1/2 cup bacon, cooked
- 1/2 cup cheddar cheese, shredded

Directions

1. Cook eggs as regular scrambled eggs. Add meat to the egg mixture while you cook, if desired.

2. Spread out puff pastry sheets on a cutting board and cut out rectangles with a cookie cutter or knife, making sure they are all uniform so they will fit nicely together.
3. Spoon preferred egg, meat, and cheese combos onto half of the pastry rectangles.
4. Place a pastry rectangle on top of the mixture and press edges together with a fork to seal.
5. Spray with spray oil if you desired a shiny, smooth pastry, but it really is optional.
6. Place breakfast pockets in the air fryer basket and cook for 8-10 minutes at 370 degrees.
7. Watch carefully and check every 2-3 minutes for desired crispness.

Nutritional Information

- Calories: 351
- Fat: 8g
- Carbs: 41g
- Protein: 25g

Flourless Broccoli Quiche

Preparation Time: 20 minutes

Yield: 2 Servings

Ingredients

- 1 Large Broccoli
- 3 Large Carrots
- 1 Large Tomato
- 100 g Cheddar Cheese grated
- 20 g Feta Cheese
- 150 ml Whole Milk
- 2 Large Eggs
- 1 Tsp Parsley
- 1 Tsp Thyme

- Salt & Pepper

Directions

1. Chop up your broccoli into florets. Peel and dice your carrots. Place your carrots and broccoli into a food steamer and cook for 20 minutes or until soft.
2. In a measuring jug add all your seasonings. Crack the eggs into the jug and mix well. Add the milk a bit at a time until you have a pale mixture.
3. When the steamer has finished drain the vegetables and line the bottom of your quiche dish with them. Layer with the tomatoes and then add your cheese on top.
4. Pour the liquid over and then add a little bit more cheese on top.
5. Place in the air fryer and cook for 20 minutes on 180c.
6. Serve.

Nutritional Information

- Calories: 340
- Fat: 24g
- Carbs: 22g
- Protein: 9g

Breakfast Style Air Fryer Potatoes

Preparation Time: 20 minutes

Yield: 4 Servings

Ingredients

- 2 medium sized Russet potatoes ~13 ounces total or roughly 2 generous cups, chopped in roughly one inch pieces
- Few generous spritzes oil spray
- Pinch salt & pepper
- 1 small bell pepper ~ 5 ounces or roughly 3/4 cup, chopped medium

- 1 small onion ~ 4 ounces or roughly 3/4 cup, chopped medium

Directions

1. Put potatoes into air fryer basket. Spritz with oil spray, shake, spritz again, and add a pinch of salt.
2. Set the air fryer to 400 degrees and ten minutes. Stop once to shake during cooking time. (Feel free to stir, if the potatoes aren't moving around enough.)
3. After the potatoes have cooked for ten minutes, add the bell pepper and onions. Add another spritz of oil, and shake basket. Set the air fryer to 400 degrees and 15 minutes.
4. During the last 5 minutes of cooking, check on the potatoes to make sure they aren't getting too brown. Depending on the size of your potatoes, you may need slightly less or slightly more time. If needed, add a few more minutes to the cooking time.
5. Add salt to taste and serve.

Nutritional Information

- Calories: 21
- Fat: 1g
- Carbs: 17g
- Protein: 3g

2. Lunches

Healthy Fish Finger Sandwich

Preparation Time: 20 minutes

Yield: 4 Servings

Ingredients

- 4 small cod fillets (skin removed)
- salt and pepper
- 2 tbsp flour
- 40g dried breadcrumbs
- spray oil
- 250g frozen peas
- 1 tbsp creme fraiche or greek yogurt
- 10-12 capers
- squeeze of lemon juice
- 4 bread rolls or 8 small slices of bread

Directions

1. Pre-heat the Air Fryer.
2. Take each of the cod fillets, season with salt and pepper and lightly dust in the flour. Then roll quickly in the breadcrumbs. The idea is to get a light coating of breadcrumbs on the fish rather than a thick layer. Repeat with each cod fillet.
3. Add a few sprays of oil spray to the bottom of the fryer basket. Place the cod fillets on top and cook on the fish setting (200c) for 15 mins.
4. Whilst the fish is cooking, cook the peas in boiling water for a couple of minutes on the hob or in the microwave. Drain and then add to a blender with the creme fraiche, capers and lemon juice to taste. Blitz until combined.
5. Once the fish has cooked, remove it from the HealthyFry Air Fryer and start layering your sandwich with the bread, fish and pea puree. You can also add lettuce, tartar sauce and any other of your favourite toppings!

Nutritional Information

- Calories: 504
- Fat: 17g
- Carbs: 67g
- Protein: 20g

Chicken Quesadillas

Preparation Time: 20 minutes

Yield: 4 Servings

Ingredients

- 2 Soft Taco Shells
- Chicken Fajita Strips
- 1/2 cup sliced green peppers

- 1/2 cup sliced onions (I use the frozen fajita blend)
- Shredded Mexican Cheese
- Salsa (optional)
- Sour Cream (optional)

Directions

1. Preheat Air Fryer on 370 degrees for about 3 minutes.
2. Spray pan lightly with vegetable oil.
3. Place 1 soft taco shell in pan.
4. Place shredded cheese on shell. (you can use as much or as little as you'd like.)
5. Lay out fajita chicken strips so they are in a single layer.
6. Put your onions and green peppers on top of your chicken.
7. Add more shredded cheese.
8. Place another soft taco shell on top and spray lightly with vegetable oil.
9. Set timer for 4 minutes.
10. Flip over carefully with large spatula.
11. Spray lightly with vegetable oil and place rack on top of shell to hold it in place.
12. Set timer for 4 minutes.
13. If it's not crispy enough for you, leave in for a couple of extra minutes.
14. Remove and cut into 4 slices or 6 slices.
15. Serve with salsa and sour cream if desired.

Nutritional Information

- Calories: 267
- Fat: 13g
- Carbs: 23g
- Protein: 15g

6 Minute Pita Bread Cheese Pizza

Preparation Time: 6 minutes

Yield: 2 Servings

Ingredients

- 1 Pita Bread
- 1 Tablespoon Pizza Sauce
- 1/4 cup Mozarella Cheese
- 1 drizzle Extra Virgin Olive Oil
- 1 Stainless Steel Short Legged Trivet

Toppings

- 7 slices Pepperoni or more
- 1/4 cup Sausage
- 1 Tablespoon Yellow/Brown Onion sliced thin
- 1/2 teaspoon Fresh Garlic minced

Directions

1. Use a spoon and swirl Pizza Sauce on to Pita Bread. Add your favorite toppings and Cheese. Add a little drizzle of Extra Virgin Olive Oil over top of Pizza.
2. Place in Air Fryer and place a Trivet over Pita Bread. Cook at 350 degrees for 6 minutes. Carefully remove from Air Fryer and cut.

Nutritional Information

- Calories: 324
- Fat: 9g
- Carbs: 40g
- Protein: 20g

Simple Cheese Sandwich

Preparation Time: 8 minutes

Yield: 1 Serving

Ingredients

- 2 slices Sandwich Bread
- 2-3 slices Cheddar Cheese
- 2 teaspoons Butter or Mayonnaise

Directions

1. Place cheese between bread slices and butter the outside of both slices of bread.
2. Place in air fryer and cook at 370 degrees for 8 minutes. Flip, halfway through.

Nutritional Information

- Calories: 430
- Fat: 17g
- Carbs: 25g
- Protein: 18g

Air Fryer Hot Dogs

Preparation Time: 10 minutes

Yield: 2 Servings

Ingredients

- 2 hot dogs
- 2 hot dog buns
- 2 tablespoons of grated cheese if desired

Directions

1. Preheat your air fryer to 390 degrees for about 4 minutes. Place two hot dogs into the air fryer, cook for about 5 minutes. Remove the hot dog from air fryer.
2. Place the hot dog on a bun, add cheese if desired.
3. Place dressed hot dog into the air fryer, and cook for an additional 2 minutes.

Nutritional Information

- Calories: 288
- Fat: 13g
- Carbs: 23g
- Protein: 12g

Bourbon Bacon Burger

Preparation Time: 30 minutes

Yield: 4 Servings

Ingredients

- 1 tablespoon bourbon
- 2 tablespoons brown sugar
- 3 strips maple bacon, cut in half
- ¾ pound ground beef (80% lean)
- 1 tablespoon minced onion
- 2 tablespoons BBQ sauce
- ½ teaspoon salt
- freshly ground black pepper
- 2 slices Colby Jack cheese (or Monterey Jack)
- 2 Kaiser rolls

- lettuce and tomato, for serving
- Zesty Burger Sauce:
- 2 tablespoons BBQ sauce
- 2 tablespoons mayonnaise
- ¼ teaspoon ground paprika
- freshly ground black pepper

Directions

1. Pre-heat the air fryer to 390°F and pour a little water into the bottom of the air fryer drawer. (This will help prevent the grease that drips into the bottom drawer from burning and smoking.)
2. Combine the bourbon and brown sugar in a small bowl. Place the bacon strips in the air fryer basket and brush with the brown sugar mixture. Air-fry at 390F for 4 minutes. Flip the bacon over, brush with more brown sugar and air-fry at 390F for an additional 4 minutes until crispy.
3. While the bacon is cooking, make the burger patties. Combine the ground beef, onion, BBQ sauce, salt and pepper in a large bowl. Mix together thoroughly with your hands and shape the meat into 2 patties.
4. Transfer the burger patties to the air fryer basket and air-fry the burgers at 370°F for 15 to 20 minutes, depending on how you like your burger cooked (15 minutes for rare to medium-rare; 20 minutes for well-done). Flip the burgers over halfway through the cooking process.
5. While the burgers are air-frying, make the burger sauce by combining the BBQ sauce, mayonnaise, paprika and freshly ground black pepper to taste in a bowl.
6. When the burgers are cooked to your liking, top each patty with a slice of Jack cheese and air-fry for an additional minute, just to melt the cheese.

7. Spread the sauce on the inside of the Kaiser rolls, place the burgers on the rolls, top with the bourbon bacon, lettuce and tomato and enjoy!

Nutritional Information

- Calories: 1060
- Fat: 65g
- Carbs: 77g
- Protein: 45g

Leftover Turkey & Cheese Calzone

Preparation Time: 10 minutes

Yield: 4 Servings

Ingredients

<u>Pizza Dough</u>

- 600 g Plain Flour
- 7 g Yeast easy blend
- 50 ml Warm Milk
- 325 ml Warm Water
- 25 ml Olive Oil
- Salt & Pepper

<u>Main</u>

- 4 Tbsp Homemade Tomato Sauce
- Leftover Turkey brown meat shredded
- 100 g Cheddar Cheese
- 25 g Mozzarella Cheese grated
- 25 g Back Bacon diced
- 1 Large Egg beaten
- 1 Tbsp Tomato Puree
- 1 Tsp Oregano
- 1 Tsp Basil
- 1 Tsp Thyme
- Salt & Pepper

Directions

1. <u>Making the dough</u> – mix the flour, yeast and salt together in a large mixing bowl and stir in the olive oil and milk. Gradually add the water, mixing well to form a soft dough. Turn the dough onto a floured workspace and knead for about five minutes, until smooth and elastic. Transfer to a clean bowl, cover with a damp tea towel and leave to rise for 90 minutes or until it has doubled in size. Knead it and repeat the process again so that it has doubled in size again. Roll out your dough and it is ready for its toppings!
2. Preheat your Air Fryer to 180c.
3. Start by rolling out your pizza dough so that they are the size of small pizzas. In a small mixing bowl add together all the seasonings as well as the tomato sauce and puree.
4. Using a cooking brush add a layer of tomato sauce to your pizza bases making sure that it doesn't actually touch the edge with a 1cm space.
5. Layer up your pizza with your turkey, bacon and cheese to one side.
6. With the 1cm gap around your pizza base and using your cooking brush again, brush with beaten egg. Fold your

pizza base over so that it resembles an uncooked Cornish pasty and all area that is now visible of the pizza dough to be brushed with more egg.
7. Place in the Air Fryer for 10 minutes at 180c.
8. Serve.

Nutritional Information

- Calories: 158
- Fat: 11g
- Carbs: 2g
- Protein: 10g

Air Fryer Chick-fil-A Nuggets

Preparation Time: 20 minutes

Yield: 6 Servings

Ingredients

- 1 cup dill pickle juice
- 1 lb boneless skinless chicken breasts, cut into pieces about 1 inch in size
- 1 egg
- 1 cup milk
- 1½ cups flour
- 3 tbsp powdered sugar
- 2 tsp salt
- 1½ tsp pepper
- ½ tsp paprika

- Olive oil spritz

Directions

1. Add chicken chunks to pickle juice and marinate in the refrigerator for about 30 minutes
2. Whisk milk and egg together and set aside
3. Combine the dry ingredients and stir, then set aside
4. Preheat air fryer to 370
5. Remove the chicken from refrigerator, drain and place each into the dry mixture, to the liquid mixture and back to the dry making sure it is well coated, making sure to shake off excess
6. Cook in a single layer of chicken for 8 minutes or until golden brown, flipping and spritzing with olive oil at the halfway mark
7. Serve with your favorite dipping sauce

Nutritional Information

- Calories: 256
- Fat: 5g
- Carbs: 29g
- Protein: 22g

Air Fried Chicken Tenders

Preparation Time: 20 minutes

Yield: 2 Servings

Ingredients

- 12oz of Chicken Breasts
- 1 Egg White
- 1/8 Cup Flour

- 35g Panko Bread Crumbs
- Salt and Pepper

Directions

1. Trim chicken breast of any excess fat and cut into tenders. Season each side with salt and pepper.
2. Dip chicken tenders into flour, then egg whites, then panko bread crumbs
3. Load into air fryer basket and spray with olive spray
4. Cook at 350 degrees for about 10 minutes or until cooked through

Nutritional Information

- Calories: 375
- Fat: 6g
- Carbs: 18g
- Protein: 57g

Roast Chicken

Preparation Time: 20 minutes

Yield: 4 Servings

Ingredients

- 4.25 pound whole chicken

Dry rub seasonings

- ¾ cup kosher salt
- ¼ cup paprika
- ¼ cup onion powder
- ¼ cup garlic powder
- ¼ cup italian seasoning
- ¼ cup brown sugar

- 2 tablespoons dried thyme
- 2 tablespoons dry mustard
- 2 tablespoons cayenne pepper
- 2 tablespoons garlic pepper

Directions

1. Clean chicken and pat dry.
2. Sprinkle generously with dry rub seasonings above.
3. Spray fry basket with cooking spray and place chicken into the basket with the legs facing down.
4. Roast chicken for 330 degrees Fahrenheit for 30 minutes.
5. Flip chicken.
6. Roast for 20 more minutes at 330 degrees Fahrenheit or until internal temperature of chicken is 165 degrees Fahrenheit.

Nutritional Information

- Calories: 311
- Fat: 20g
- Carbs: 8g
- Protein: 29g

Best Air Fryer Cookbook for Beginners

3. Appetizers and Sides

Beetroot Chips

Preparation Time: 20 minutes

Yield: 4 Servings

Ingredients

- 2 Medium Sized Beetroot
- 1/2 Tsp Oil
- Salt to taste
- Pepper Optional

Directions

1. Wash the Beetroot, peel the skin and set the skin aside. Using a mandoline slicer, slice them thin. Alternatively, if you don't have a slicer, slice them uniformly thin with your knife.
2. Spread the beetroot slices on the paper and place another paper on top of it. Keep it aside for 10 minutes. This process will enable to absorb any extra moisture on the beetroot thins.
3. Sprinkle the required amount of salt on the beetroot.
4. Preheat the Airfryer to 150 C for 4 minutes. Pull the basket from the air fryer and place the chips in them. Slide it back in the air fryer and fry for 15 minutes. Make sure to remove in between after every 5 minutes and give it a good shake. Once the chips are slightly crisp on the outer edges and tender in the middle, allow them to cool down for some time.
5. Slide the basket with the chips back again and heat at 180 C for another 3 minutes. The chips will be really crisp overall and perfect to munch right away.
6. Season with Sea Salt and freshly ground pepper if you like or just munch it as it is. We love it either way.

Nutritional Information

- Calories: 150
- Fat: 8g
- Carbs: 20g
- Protein: 4g

Air-Fried Shishito Peppers

Preparation Time: 10 minutes

Yield: 4 Servings

Ingredients

- 16 oz bag Shishito peppers
- salt and pepper to taste
- 1/2 tbsp avocado oil

- 1/3 cup Asiagio Cheese grated fine
- Limes

Directions

1. Rinse peppers with water and pat dry with paper towel. Place in bowl and toss with avocado oil, salt, and pepper. Place in air fryer and cook at 350 for 10 minutes. Watch carefully. You want them to come out blistered looking but not burnt.
2. Place shishito peppers on serving platter. Drizzle with a little lime juice and top with grated asiago cheese. Serve!

Nutritional Information

- Calories: 63
- Fat: 4g
- Carbs: 1g
- Protein: 3g

Air-Fryer French Fries

Preparation Time: 20 minutes

Yield: 2 Servings

Ingredients

- 3 medium potatoes, whole, unpeeled
- 1/4 teaspoon garlic powder/ granulated garlic
- salt and pepper to taste
- 1 1/2 tablespoons oil of choice (Coconut also works well.)

Directions

1. Wash your potatoes, and pat them dry.
2. Slice your potatoes to the size fries you want, and try to be somewhat consistent with the size to allow for even cooking. (Note: larger fries may require slightly more cook time.)
3. Toss your fries with the oil, garlic, salt and pepper. You can toss them in a bowl, or toss them in your air fryer basket.
4. Cook them on 400 in the air fryer for about 20 minutes (more for larger, steak fries), and toss them around a couple times during the cooking to help evenly cook.
5. Taste to see if you need more salt and pepper.

Nutritional Information

- Calories: 278
- Fat: 10g
- Carbs: 40g
- Protein: 8g

Coconut Shrimp With Spicy Marmalade Sauce

Preparation Time: 20 minutes

Yield: 2 Servings

Ingredients

- 8 large shrimp shelled and deveined
- 8 ounces coconut milk
- 1/2 cup shredded sweetened coconut
- 1/2 cup panko bread
- 1/2 teaspoon cayenner pepper
- 1/4 teaspoon kosher salt
- 1/4 teaspoon fresh ground pepper
- 1/2 cup orange marmalade
- 1 tablespoon honey
- 1 teaspoon mustard
- 1/4 teaspoon hot sauce

Directions

1. Clean the shrimp and set aside.
2. In a small bowl, whisk the coconut milk and season with salt and pepper. Set aside. In a separate small bowl, whisk together the coconut, panko, cayenne pepper, salt and pepper.
3. One at a time, dip the shrimp in the coconut milk, the panko and then place in the basket of the fryer. Repeat until all the shrimp are coated. Cook the shrimp in the fryer for 20 minutes at 350 degrees or until the shrimp are cooked through.
4. While the shrimp are cooking, whisk together the marmalade, honey, mustard and hot sauce.
5. Serve the shrimp with the sauce immediately.

Nutritional Information

- Calories: 623
- Fat: 21g
- Carbs: 76g
- Protein: 15g

Air Fryer Baked Sweet Potato

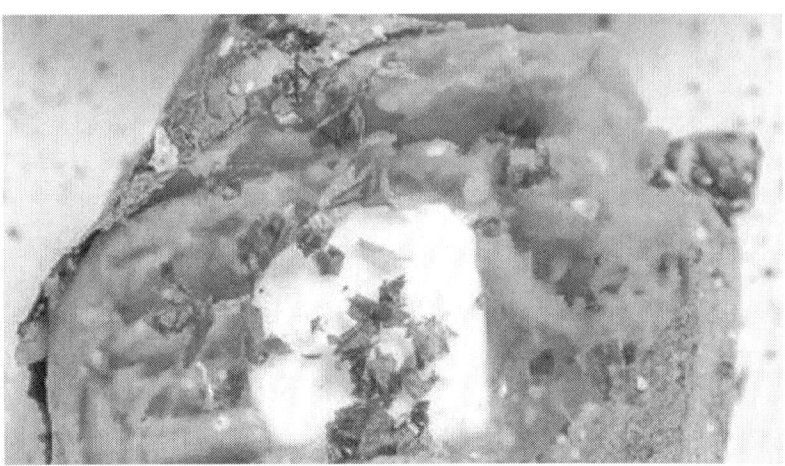

Preparation Time: 40 minutes

Yield: 3 Servings

Ingredients

- 3 sweet potatoes
- 1 tablespoon olive oil
- 1-2 teaspoons kosher salt

Directions

1. Wash your sweet potatoes and then create air holes with a fork in the potatoes.
2. Sprinkle them with the olive oil & salt, then rub evenly on the potatoes.

3. Once the potatoes are coated place them into the basket for the Air Fryer and place into the machine.
4. Cook your potatoes at 392 degrees for 35-40 minutes or until fork tender.
5. Top with your favorites!

Nutritional Information

- Calories: 152
- Fat: 4g
- Carbs: 26g
- Protein: 2g

Jalapeño Poppers

Preparation Time: 20 minutes

Yield: 4 Servings

Ingredients

- 10 jalapeno peppers halved and deseeded
- 8 oz of cream cheese (you can use a dairy-free cream cheese)
- 1/4 c fresh parsley
- 3/4 c gluten-free tortilla or bread crumbs

Directions

1. Mix together 1/2 of crumbs and cream cheese. Once combined add in the parsley.
2. Stuff each pepper with this mixture.
3. Gently press the tops of the peppers into the remaining 1/4 c of crumbs to create the top coating.
4. Cook in an air fryer at 370 degrees F for 6-8 minutes OR in a conventional oven at 375 degrees F for 20 minutes.
5. Let cool and ENJOY!

Nutritional Information

- Calories: 152
- Fat: 10g
- Carbs: 45g
- Protein: 4g

Pork Taquitos

Preparation Time: 20 minutes

Yield: 2 Servings

Ingredients

- 3 cups cooked shredded pork tenderloin or chicken
- 2 1/2 cups fat free shredded mozzarella
- 10 small flour tortillas

- 1 lime, juiced
- Cooking spray

Directions

1. Preheat air fryer to 380 degrees.
2. Sprinkle lime juice over pork and gently mix around.
3. Microwave 5 tortillas at a time with a damp paper towel over it for 10 seconds, to soften.
4. Add 3 oz. of pork and 1/4 cup of cheese to a tortilla.
5. Tightly and gently roll up the tortillas.
6. Line tortillas on a greased foil lined pan.
7. Spray an even coat of cooking spray over tortillas.
8. Air Fry for 7-10 minutes until tortillas are a golden color, flipping half way through.
9. 2 taquitos per serving.

Nutritional Information

- Calories: 256
- Fat: 4g
- Carbs: 23g
- Protein: 31g

Taco Bell Crunch Wraps

Preparation Time: 20 minutes

Yield: 4 Servings

Ingredients

- 2 lbs ground beef
- 2 Tbps. Taco Seasoning
- 1 1/3 c water
- 6 flour tortillas, 12 inch
- 3 roma tomatoes
- 12 oz nacho cheese
- 2 c lettuce, shredded
- 2 c Mexican blend cheese
- 2 c sour cream
- 6 tostadas
- Olive oil or butter spray

Directions

1. Preheat air fryer to 400
2. Prepare ground beef according to taco seasoning packet
3. In the center of each flour tortilla with 2/3 c of beef, 4 tbs of nacho cheese, 1 tostada, 1/3 c sour cream, 1/3 c of lettuce. 1/6th of the tomatoes and 1/3 c cheese
4. To close, flood the edges up, over the center, it should look sort of like a pinwheel
5. Repeat 2 and 3 with remaining wraps
6. Lay seam side down in your air fryer
7. Spray with oil
8. Cook for 2 mins or until brown
9. Using a spatula, carefully flip and spray again
10. Cook an additional 2 mins and repeat with remaining wraps
11. Allow to cool a few mins and enjoy.

Nutritional Information

- Calories: 954
- Fat: 30g
- Carbs: 34g
- Protein: 42g

Panko Breaded Chicken Parmesan With Marinara Sauce

Preparation Time: 30 minutes

Yield: 4 Servings

Ingredients

- 16 oz skinless chicken breasts sliced in half to make 4 breasts
- 1 cup panko bread crumbs
- 1/2 cup parmesan cheese grated
- 1/2 cup mozarella cheese shredded
- 1/8 cup egg whites
- 3/4 cup marinara sauce

- 2 tsp Italian seasoning
- salt and pepper to taste
- cooking spray

Directions

1. Preheat the Air Fryer to 400. Spray the basket with cooking spray.
2. Slice the chicken breasts in half horizontally to create 4 thinner chicken breasts. Place the chicken breasts on a hard surface and pound them to completely flatten.
3. Grate the parmesan cheese.
4. Combine the panko breadcrumbs, cheese, and seasonings in a bowl large enough to dip the chicken breasts. Stir to combine.
5. Place the egg whites in a bowl large enough to dip the chicken.
6. Dip the chicken in the egg whites and then the breadcrumbs mixture.
7. Place in the Air Fryer. Spray the top of the chicken with cooking spray.
8. Cook for 7 minutes. Top each of the breasts with marinara sauce and the shredded mozzarella. Cook for an additional 3 minutes or until cheese has melted.

Nutritional Information

- Calories: 332
- Fat: 12g
- Carbs: 13g
- Protein: 37g

Apple Cinnamon Dessert Empanadas

Preparation Time: 30 minutes

Yield: 12 Servings

Ingredients

- 12 empanada wrappers
- 2 apples diced, I used one red and 1 green
- 2 tbsp raw honey

- 1 tsp vanilla extract
- 1 tsp cinnamon
- 1/8 tsp nutmeg
- 1 tsp olive oil spray
- 2 tsp cornstarch
- 1 tsp water

Directions

1. Place a saucepan on medium-high heat. Add the apples, cinnamon, nutmeg, honey, and vanilla. Stir and cook for 2-3 minutes until the apples are soft.
2. Mix the cornstarch and water in a small bowl. Add to the pan and stir. Cook for 30 seconds.
3. Lay the empanada wrappers on a flat surface. Add the apple mixture to each.
4. Close the empanadas. Roll the empanada in half. Pinch the crust along each of the edges. Roll each of the sides inward. Continue to twist the crust until closed.
5. Add the empanadas to the Air Fryer basket. It's ok to stack the empanadas.
6. Place the Air Fryer on 400 degrees. Cook for 8 minutes.
7. Turn and flip the empanadas. Cook for an additional 10 minutes.
8. Cool before serving.

Nutritional Information

- Calories: 164
- Fat: 5g
- Carbs: 28g
- Protein: 3g

4. Fish and Seafoods

3 Ingredient Fried Catfish

Preparation Time: 60 minutes

Yield: 4 Servings

Ingredients

- 4 catfish fillets
- 1/4 cup seasoned fish fry

- 1 tbsp olive oil
- 1 tbsp chopped parsley optional

Directions

1. Preheat Air Fryer to 400 degrees.
2. Rinse the catfish and pat dry.
3. Pour the fish fry seasoning in a large Ziploc bag.
4. Add the catfish to the bag, one at a time. Seal the bag and shake. Ensure the entire filet is coated with seasoning.
5. Spray olive oil on the top of each filet.
6. Place the filet in the Air Fryer basket. (Due to the size of my fillets, I cooked each one at a time). Close and cook for 10 minutes.
7. Flip the fish. Cook for an additional 10 minutes.
8. Flip the fish.
9. Cook for an additional 2-3 minutes or until desired crispness.
10. Top with parsley.

Nutritional Information

- Calories: 208
- Fat: 6g
- Carbs: 8g
- Protein: 17g

Crumbed Fish

Preparation Time: 20 minutes

Yield: 4 Servings

Ingredients

- 4 tablespoons vegetable oil
- 100g breadcrumbs
- 1 egg, whisked
- 4 fish fillets
- 1 lemon, to serve

Directions

1. Preheat your air fryer to 180 degrees C.
2. Mix the oil and the breadcrumbs together. Keep stirring until the mixture becomes loose and crumbly.
3. Dip the fish fillets into the egg then shake of any residual. Dip the fish fillets into the crumb mix making sure it is evenly and fully covered.
4. Gently lay in the air fryer then cook for 12 minutes. (Time may vary depending on the thickness of the fish).
5. Serve immediately with lemon.

Nutritional Information

- Calories: 148
- Fat: 7g
- Carbs: 13g
- Protein: 7g

Cajun Salmon

Preparation Time: 15 minutes

Yield: 2 Servings

Ingredients

- 1 piece fresh salmon fillet (about 200g)
- Cajun seasoning (just enough to coat)
- A light sprinkle of sugar (optional)
- Juice from a quarter of lemon, to serve

Directions

1. Preheat your airfryer to 180C. For the Philips airfryer, the orange light will go off to indicate that the temperature has been reached. For other brands, typically just preheat for 5 minutes.

2. Clean your salmon and pat dry. In a plate, sprinkle Cajun seasoning all over and ensure all sides are coated. You don't need too much. If you prefer a tad of sweetness, add a light sprinkling of sugar. NO seasoning time required.
3. For a salmon fillet about 3/4 of an inch thick, airfry for 7 minutes, skin side up on the grill pan. Serve immediately with a squeeze of lemon.

Nutritional Information

- Calories: 200
- Fat: 12g
- Carbs: 1g
- Protein: 22g

Crunchy Air Fryer Sushi Roll

Preparation Time: 10 minutes

Yield: 3 Servings

Ingredients

For the Kale Salad

- 1 1/2 cups chopped kale - ribs removed
- 1/2 teaspoon rice vinegar
- 3/4 teaspoon toasted sesame oil
- 1/8 teaspoon garlic powder
- 1/4 teaspoon ground ginger
- 3/4 teaspoon soy sauce
- 1 tablespoon sesame seeds - toasted or not - your call!

For the Kale Salad Sushi Rolls

- 1 batch Pressure Cooker Sushi Rice, cooked - cooled to room temperature
- 3 sheets of sushi nori
- 1/2 of a Haas avocado - sliced

Make the Sriracha Mayo

- 1/4 cup of your favorite vegan mayonnaise – (I used Vegenaise.)
- sriracha sauce - to taste

For the Coating

- 1/2 cup panko breadcrumbs

Directions

Make the Kale Salad

- In a large bowl, combine the kale, vinegar, sesame oil, garlic powder, ground ginger, and soy sauce. With clean hands, massage the kale until it turns bright green and wilted. Stir in the sesame seeds, and set aside.

Make the Kale Salad Sushi Rolls

- Lay out a sheet of nori on a dry surface. With slightly damp fingertips, grab a handful of rice, and spread it onto the nori. The idea here is to get a thin layer of rice covering almost the entire sheet. Along one edge, you'll want to leave about 1/2" of naked seaweed. Think of this as the flap that will seal your roll shut.
- On the end of the seaweed opposite that naked part, lay out about 2-3 tablespoons of kale salad, and top with a couple of slices of avocado. Starting on the end with the filling, roll up your sushi, pressing gently to get a nice,

tight roll. When you get to the end, use that naked bit of seaweed to seal the roll closed. If needed, get your fingertips wet, and moisten that bit of seaweed to make it stick.
- Repeat steps 2-3 to make 3 more sushi rolls.

Make the Sriracha Mayo

- In a shallow bowl, whisk together the vegan mayo with sriracha, until you reach the heat level that you like. Start with 1 teaspoon, and add more, 1/2 teaspoon at a time, until you have the spicy mayo of your dreams!

Fry and Slice

- Pour the panko breadcrumbs into a shallow bowl.
- Grab your first sushi roll, and coat it as evenly as possible in the Sriracha Mayo, then in the panko. Place the roll into your air fryer basket. Repeat with the rest of your sushi rolls.
- Air fry at 390F for 10 minutes, shaking gently after 5 minutes.
- When the rolls are cool enough to handle, grab a good knife, and very gently slice the roll into 6-8 pieces. When you're slicing, think of gently sawing, and don't press hard with your knife. That will just send kale and avocado flying out of the ends of your roll.
- Serve with soy sauce for dipping.

Nutritional Information

- Calories: 140
- Fat: 2g
- Carbs: 23g
- Protein: 7g

BANG BANG Fried Shrimp

Preparation Time: 20 minutes

Yield: 4 Servings

Ingredients

- 1 pound raw shrimp peeled and deveined
- 1 egg white 3 tbsp
- 1/2 cup all purpose flour
- 3/4 cup panko bread crumbs
- 1 tsp paprika
- McCormick's Grill Mates Montreal Chicken Seasoning to taste
- salt and pepper to taste
- cooking spray
- Bang Bang Sauce
- 1/3 cup plain, non-fat Greek yogurt
- 2 tbsp Sriracha

- 1/4 cup sweet chili sauce

Directions

1. Preheat Air Fryer to 400 degrees.
2. Season the shrimp with the seasonings.
3. Place the flour, egg whites, and panko bread crumbs in three separate bowls.
4. Create a cooking station. Dip the shrimp in the flour, then the egg whites, and the panko bread crumbs last.
5. When dipping the shrimp in the egg whites, you do not need to submerge the shrimp. Do a light dab so that most of the flour stays on the shrimp. You want the egg white to adhere to the panko crumbs.
6. Spray the shrimp with cooking spray. Do not spray directly on the shrimp. The panko will go flying. Keep a nice distance.
7. Add the shrimp to the Air Fryer basket. Cook for 4 minutes. Open the basket and flip the shrimp to the other side. Cook for an additional 4 minutes or until crisp.

Bang Bang Sauce

8. Combine all of the ingredients in a small bowl. Mix thoroughly to combine.

Nutritional Information

- Calories: 242
- Fat: 1g
- Carbs: 32g
- Protein: 37g

Airfried Salmon Patties

Preparation Time: 30 minutes

Yield: 4 Servings

Ingredients

- 3 large russet potatoes (about 400g total)
- 1 salmon portion (about 200g)
- A handful of frozen vegetables (parboiled and drained)

- Chopped parsley
- 2 sprinkles of dill
- A few dashes of black pepper
- Salt to taste
- 1 egg
- Breadcrumbs to coat (you can use packaged panko or blend 4 pieces bread)
- Olive oil spray

Directions

1. Peel and chop potatoes into small pieces. Bring a pot of water to boil and cook potatoes for about 10 minutes or til tender. Remove water and return potatoes to the pot on low flame. Let the water evaporate (about 2-3 minutes), taking care not to burn the potatoes. Mash with a whisk and transfer to a large mixing bowl. Refrigerate til no longer hot.
2. In the meantime, prepare your breadcrumbs if not using packaged panko. Blend 4 pieces til fine but not overly so. Set aside.
3. Airfry the salmon. Preheat AF for 5 minutes at 180C, then grill salmon for 5 minutes. Flake with a fork and set aside.
4. Remove mash potatoes from fridge and add parboiled vegetables, flaked salmon, chopped parsley, black pepper, dill and salt. Do a taste test since everything is already cooked, and adjust seasonings to your liking. Add the egg and combine everything together.
5. With dry hands, shape into 6-8 patties or smaller balls. Coat with breadcrumbs, spray some oil (make sure the breadcrumbs get oil on them if not the colour won't be nice), and AF at 180C til golden (about 10-12 minutes). If using the grill pan, there is no need to line with aluminium foil like I did. If lining with foil, you need to flip halfway once the top is golden.

6. Serve with mayo and lemon with a salad on the side.

Nutritional Information

- Calories: 229
- Fat: 8g
- Carbs: 11g
- Protein: 26g

Honey-Glazed Salmon

Preparation Time: 20 minutes

Yield: 4 Servings

Ingredients

- 2 pcs Salmon Fillets (about 100gm each)
- 6 tbsp Honey
- 6 tsp Soy Sauce
- 3 tsp Rice Wine Vinegar
- 1 tsp Water

Directions

1. Mix honey, soy sauce, rice wine and water together.
2. Pour half (or some) of the mixture in a separate bowl, set aside as this will be used as sauce to serve with the salmon.
3. Put together the salmon and the marinade mixture, let it marinate for at least 2 hours.
4. Pre-heat the Airfryer at 180°C.
5. Air-grilled the salmon for 8 minutes, flip over halfway and continue with additional 5 minutes. Baste the salmon with the marinade mixture every 3 minutes.
6. To prepare the sauce, pour the remaining sauce in a pan and let it simmer for 1 minutes. Serve with salmon.

Nutritional Information

- Calories: 414
- Fat: 23g
- Carbs: 20g
- Protein: 34g

Henry Wilson

Cajun Shrimp

Preparation Time: 10 minutes

Yield: 4 Servings

Ingredients

- 1/2 pound tiger shrimp (16-20 count)

- ¼ teaspoon cayenne pepper
- ½ teaspoon old bay seasoning
- ¼ teaspoon smoked paprika
- 1 pinch of salt
- 1 tablespoon olive oil

Directions

1. Preheat the air fryer to 390°F. In a mixing bowl, combine all of the ingredients, coating the shrimp with the oil and the spices.
2. Place the shrimp into the cooking basket and cook for 5 minutes.
3. Serve over rice.

Nutritional Information

- Calories: 457
- Fat: 10g
- Carbs: 51g
- Protein: 37g

Henry Wilson

Spicy Fish Street Tacos with Sriracha Slaw

Preparation Time: 20 minutes

Yield: 2 Servings

Ingredients

Sriracha Slaw:

- ½ cup mayonnaise
- 2 tablespoons rice vinegar
- 1 teaspoon sugar
- 2 tablespoons sriracha chili sauce
- 5 cups shredded green cabbage
- ¼ cup shredded carrots
- 2 scallions, chopped
- salt and freshly ground black pepper

Tacos:

- ½ cup flour
- 1 teaspoon chili powder
- ½ teaspoon ground cumin
- 1 teaspoon salt
- freshly ground black pepper
- ½ teaspoon baking powder
- 1 egg, beaten
- ¼ cup milk
- 1 cup breadcrumbs
- 12 ounces mahi-mahi or snapper fillets
- 1 tablespoon canola or vegetable oil
- 6 (6-inch) flour tortillas
- 1 lime, cut into wedges

Directions

1. Start by making the sriracha slaw. Combine the mayonnaise, rice vinegar, sugar, and sriracha sauce in a large bowl. Mix well and add the green cabbage, carrots, and scallions. Toss until all the vegetables are coated with the dressing and season with salt and pepper. Refrigerate the slaw until you are ready to serve the tacos.

2. Combine the flour, chili powder, cumin, salt, pepper and baking powder in a bowl. Add the egg and milk and mix until the batter is smooth. Place the breadcrumbs in shallow dish.
3. Cut the fish fillets into 1-inch wide sticks, approximately 4-inches long. You should have about 12 fish sticks total. Dip the fish sticks into the batter, coating all sides. Let the excess batter drip off the fish and then roll them in the breadcrumbs, patting the crumbs onto all sides of the fish sticks. Set the coated fish on a plate or baking sheet until all the fish has been coated.
4. Pre-heat the air fryer to 400°F.
5. Spray the coated fish sticks with oil on all sides. Spray or brush the inside of the air fryer basket with oil and transfer the fish to the basket. Place as many sticks as you can in one layer, leaving a little room around each stick. Place any remaining sticks on top, perpendicular to the first layer.
6. Air-fry the fish for 3 minutes. Turn the fish sticks over and air fry for an additional 2 minutes.
7. While the fish is air-frying, warm the tortilla shells either in a 350°F oven wrapped in foil or in a skillet with a little oil over medium-high heat for a couple minutes. Fold the tortillas in half and keep them warm until the remaining tortillas and fish are ready.
8. To assemble the tacos, place two pieces of the fish in each tortilla shell and top with the sriracha slaw. Squeeze the lime wedge over top and dig in.

Nutritional Information

- Calories: 192
- Fat: 36g
- Carbs: 20g
- Protein: 17g

Zesty Ranch Air Fryer Fish Fillets

Preparation Time: 12 minutes

Yield: 4 Servings

Ingredients

- 3/4 cup bread crumbs or Panko or crushed cornflakes
- 1 30g packet dry ranch-style dressing mix
- 2 1/2 tablespoons vegetable oil
- 2 eggs beaten
- 4 tilapia salmon or other fish fillets
- lemon wedges to garnish

Directions

1. Preheat your air fryer to 180 degrees C.
2. Mix the panko/breadcrumbs and the ranch dressing mix together. Add in the oil and keep stirring until the mixture becomes loose and crumbly.
3. Dip the fish fillets into the egg, letting the excess drip off.
4. Dip the fish fillets into the crumb mixture, making sure to coat them evenly and thoroughly.
5. Place into your air fryer carefully.
6. Cook for 12-13 minutes, depending on the thickness of the fillets.
7. Remove and serve. Squeeze the lemon wedges over the fish if desired.

Nutritional Information

- Calories: 315
- Fat: 14g
- Carbs: 8g
- Protein: 49g

Best Air Fryer Cookbook for Beginners

5. Poultry Recipes

Chicken Parmesan

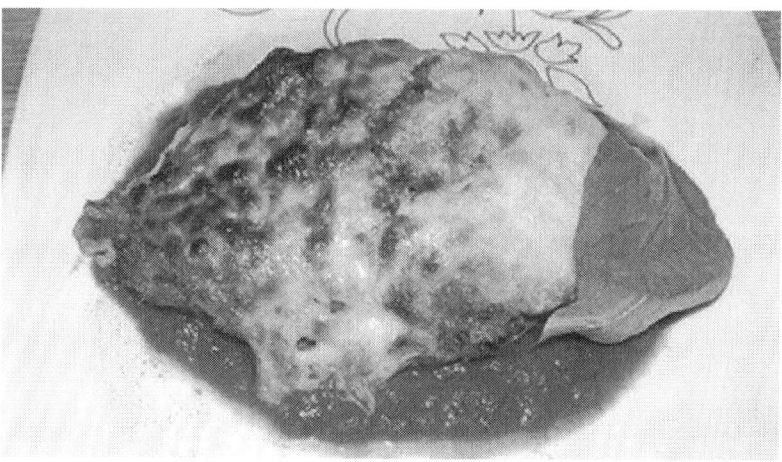

Preparation Time: 12 minutes

Yield: 4 Servings

Ingredients

- 2 (about 8 oz each) chicken breast, sliced in half to make 4 thinner cutlets
- 6 tbsp seasoned breadcrumbs
- 2 tbsp grated Parmesan cheese

- 1 tbsp butter, melted (or olive oil)
- 6 tbsp reduced fat mozzarella cheese
- 1/2 cup marinara
- cooking spray

Directions

1. Preheat the air fryer 360F° for 9 minutes. Spray the basked lightly with spray.
2. Combine breadcrumbs and parmesan cheese in a bowl. Melt the butter in another bowl.
3. Lightly brush the butter onto the chicken, then dip into breadcrumb mixture.
4. When the air fryer is ready, place 2 pieces in the basket and spray the top with oil.
5. Cook 6 minutes, turn and top each with 1 tbsp sauce and 1 1/2 tbsp of shredded mozzarella cheese.
6. Cook 3 more minutes or until cheese is melted.
7. Set aside and keep warm, repeat with the remaining 2 pieces.

Nutritional Information

- Calories: 251
- Fat: 10g
- Carbs: 14g
- Protein: 31g

Air Fryer Sriracha-Honey Chicken Wings

Preparation Time: 12 minutes

Yield: 4 Servings

Ingredients

- 1 pound chicken wings, tips removed and wings cut into individual drummettes and flats.
- 1/4 cup honey
- 2 tablespoons sriracha sauce
- 1 1/2 tablespoons soy sauce
- 1 tablespoon butter
- juice of 1/2 lime
- cilantro, chives, or scallions for garnish

Directions

1. Preheat the air fryer to 360 degrees F. Add the chicken wings to the air fryer basket, and cook for 30 minutes, turning the chicken about every 7 minutes with tongs to make sure the wings are evenly browned.
2. While the wings are cooking, add the sauce ingredients to a small sauce pan and bring to a boil for about 3 minutes.
3. When the wings are cooked, toss them in a bowl with the sauce until fully coated, sprinkle with the garnish, and serve immediately.

Nutritional Information

- Calories: 303
- Fat: 14g
- Carbs: 23g
- Protein: 18g

Tandoori Chicken

Preparation Time: 30 minutes

Yield: 4 Servings

Ingredients

- Chicken leg With Thigh - 4

For the first Marinade

- Ginger paste - 3 tsp
- Garlic paste - 3 tsp
- Salt to taste
- Lemon juice - 3 tbsp

For the second Marinade

- Tandoori masala powder - 2 tbsp
- Roasted cumin powder - 1 tsp
- Garam masala powder - 1 tsp
- Red chili powder - 2 tsp
- Turmeric powder - 1 tsp
- Hung curd - 4 tbsp
- Orange food color - a pinch optional
- Kasuri Methi - 2 tsp
- Black pepper powder - 1 tsp
- Coriander powder - 2 tsp
- Notes - You can add a bit of Mustard oil to the second marinade to get the Pungent taste in the chicken if you wish.

Directions

1. Wash the chicken legs and make slits in them using a sharp knife.
2. Add chicken in a bowl along with the ingredients for the first marinade.
3. Mix well and keep aside for 15 minutes.
4. Mix the ingredients for the second marinade and pour them over the chicken.
5. Mix well.
6. Cover the bowl and refrigerate for at least 10-12 hours.
7. Line the basket of the air fryer with aluminium foil.

8. Pre heat to 230 degrees C.
9. Place the chicken on the basket and air fry for 18-20 minutes, until slightly charred and browned.
10. Serve hot with Yogurt mint dip and Onion rings.

Nutritional Information

- Calories: 178
- Fat: 6g
- Carbs: 2g
- Protein: 25g

Zinger Chicken Burger

Preparation Time: 12 minutes

Yield: 4 Servings

Ingredients

- 6 Chicken Breasts
- 1 Small Egg beaten
- 50 g Plain Flour
- 10 ml KFC Spice Blend
- 100 ml Bread Crumbs
- 1 Tsp Worcester Sauce
- 1 Tsp Mustard Powder
- 1 Tsp Paprika
- Salt & Pepper

Directions

1. Mince your chicken in the food processor. In the food processor add your Worcester sauce, mustard, paprika and salt and pepper. Make your chicken into burger shapes and put them to one side.
2. In one bowl have your egg; in another add your flour. In a third have your KFC spice blend mix with your bread crumbs.
3. Cover your Zinger burgers in the flour, the egg and then the bread crumbs.
4. Place in the Airfryer at 180c for 15 minutes or until the chicken is cooked in the centre.

Nutritional Information

- Calories: 549
- Fat: 11g
- Carbs: 28g
- Protein: 78g

Garlic Parmesan Chicken Wings

Preparation Time: 20 minutes

Yield: 12 Servings

Ingredients

- 2 lbs wings + drumettes
- 3/4 cup grated parmesan cheese

- 2 tsps minced garlic
- 2 tsps fresh parsley, chopped
- 1 tsp salt
- 1 tsp pepper

Directions

1. Preheat your air fryer to 400 degrees for 3-4 minutes
2. Pat chicken pieces dry with a paper towel.
3. Mix parmesan cheese, garlic, parsley, salt and pepper together in a bowl.
4. Toss chicken pieces in cheese mixture until coated.
5. Place chicken in the bottom of the air fryer basket and set timer to 12 minutes.
6. After 12 minutes, use tongs to flip chicken.
7. Fry again for 12 minutes.
8. Remove chicken from basket with tongs and sprinkle with more parmesan cheese and parsley.
9. Serve with ranch, buffalo, or your favorite dipping sauce.

Nutritional Information

- Calories: 239
- Fat: 20g
- Carbs: 10g
- Protein: 13g

Air Fryer Rotisserie Chicken

Preparation Time: 12 minutes

Yield: 4 Servings

Ingredients

Brine:

- 1 Chicken OXO Cube
- 1 Tbsp Paprika
- 2 Tsp Thyme
- Salt & Pepper

Chicken Rub:

- 1 Tbsp Olive Oil
- 1 Tbsp Paprika
- 1 Tsp Celery Salt
- Salt & Pepper

Directions

1. Place all of your brine ingredients into your freezer bag. Add the whole chicken and then fill with cold water until the chicken is fully covered. Zip it up and refridgerate it overnight.
2. The next day when you are ready to cook your Air Fryer Rotisserie Chicken remove the chicken from the bag, remove the giblets, remove the brine stock and pat dry your whole chicken with some kitchen towel.
3. Make your chicken rub in a small bowl.
4. Place your whole chicken in the Air Fryer (breast side down) and rub ½ of the olive oil and ½ of the chicken rub into all visible skin.
5. Cook the chicken for 20 minutes at 180c/360f.
6. After 20 minutes turn over with kitchen tongs, then add the remainder of the oil and the chicken rub onto the other side of the chicken.
7. Now cook for a further 20 minutes at the same temperature.
8. Serve warm.

Nutritional Information

- Calories: 369
- Fat: 17g
- Carbs: 1g
- Protein: 52g

Air-Fryer Garlic Parmesan Chicken Tenders

Preparation Time: 12 minutes

Yield: 4 Servings

Ingredients

- 8 chicken tenders, raw
- 1 egg
- 2 tablespoons of water
- canola or non-fat cooking spray

For the dredge coating:

- 1 cup panko breadcrumbs
- 1/2 tsp salt
- 1/4 tsp ground black pepper, more or less to taste
- 1 tsp garlic powder

- 1/2 tsp onion powder
- 1/4 cup parmesan cheese

Directions

1. Combine the dredge coating ingredients in a bowl big enough to fit the chicken pieces.
2. In a second bowl large enough for dredging, place egg and water and whisk to combine.
3. Dip chicken tenders into the egg wash and then into the panko dredge mixture.
4. Place the breaded tenders into the fry basket. Repeat with remaining tenders.
5. Place the Fry Basket into the Power Air Fryer XL.
6. Spray a light coat of canola oil of non-fat cooking spray over the panko.
7. Press the M button. Scroll to the French Fries Icon.
8. Press the Power Button. Adjust cooking time to 12 minutes at 400 degrees.
9. Halfway through cooking, flip the tenders over.
10. Notes: For best results, do not skip coating the chicken with your favorite cooking spray or turning them halfway through cooking.

Nutritional Information

- Calories: 220
- Fat: 12g
- Carbs: 6g
- Protein: 27g

Air Fryer Pizza Stuffed Chicken

Preparation Time: 15 minutes

Yield: 2 Servings

Ingredients

- 5 boneless skinless, chicken thighs
- 1/2 cup pizza sauce
- 14 slices turkey pepperoni
- 1/2 small red onion sliced
- 5 oz sliced mozzarella cheese
- 1/2 cup shredded cheese for topping

Directions

1. Open your chicken thighs and lay them flat on a piece of parchment paper.
2. Place a second piece of parchment paper over the chicken.
3. Pound the chicken to create a thin piece. This makes the chicken easier to fold, and cook quickly. Spoon on a tablespoon of pizza sauce on each piece of chicken and spread it evenly.
4. Place 3 pieces of turkey pepperoni on top of the sauce.
5. Add one slice of Mozzarella cheese.
6. Fold one side of the chicken over on to the other
7. Use a toothpick or skewer stick to hold the chicken together. Once cooked it stays together on its own.
8. Preheat the air fryer at 370F for 2 minutes.
9. Grease the tray, and lay the pieces out in a single layer.
10. Add the chicken and let it cook for 6 minutes.
11. Flip and cook for another 6 minutes.
12. For the last 3 minutes, add cheese to melt on the top. Cooktime may vary depending on how thick your chicken pieces are. Always check chicken thighs to ensure they are heated to 165F.

Nutritional Information

- Calories: 195
- Fat: 6g
- Carbs: 3g
- Protein: 31g

Air-Fryer Thai Peanut Chicken Egg Rolls

Preparation Time: 15 minutes

Yield: 4 Servings

Ingredients

- 4 egg roll wrappers
- 2 c. rotisserie chicken shredded
- 1/4 c. Thai peanut sauce
- 1 medium carrot very thinly sliced or ribboned
- 3 green onions chopped
- 1/4 red bell pepper julienned
- non-stick cooking spray or sesame oil

Directions

1. Preheat Airfryer to 390° or oven to 425°.
2. In a small bowl, toss the chicken with the Thai peanut sauce.
3. Lay the egg roll wrappers out on a clean dry surface. Over the bottom third of an egg roll wrapper, arrange 1/4 the carrot, bell pepper and onions. Spoon 1/2 cup of the chicken mixture over the vegetables.
4. Moisten the outside edges of the wrapper with water. Fold the sides of the wrapper toward the center and roll tightly.
5. Repeat with remaining wrappers. (Keep remaining wrappers covered with a damp paper towel until ready to use.)
6. Spray the assembled egg rolls with non-stick cooking spray. Turn them over and spray the back sides as well.
7. Place the egg rolls in the Airfryer and bake at 390° for 6-8 minutes or until they are crispy and golden brown.
8. (If you are baking the egg rolls in an oven, place the seam side down on a baking sheet coated with cooking spray. Bake at 425° for 15-20 minutes.)
9. Slice in half and serve with additional Thai peanut sauce for dipping.

Nutritional Information

- Calories: 235
- Fat: 7g
- Carbs: 17g
- Protein: 21g

Air Fryer Chicken Nuggets

Preparation Time: 20 minutes

Yield: 4 Servings

Ingredients

- 16 oz (2 large) skinless boneless chicken breasts, cut into even 1-inch bite sized pieces
- 1/2 teaspoon kosher salt and black pepper, to taste
- 2 teaspoons olive oil
- 6 tablespoons whole wheat Italian seasoned breadcrumbs
- 2 tablespoons panko
- 2 tablespoons grated parmesan cheese
- olive oil spray

Directions

1. Preheat air fryer to 400°F for 8 minutes.
2. Put the olive oil in one bowl and the breadcrumbs, panko and parmesan cheese in another.
3. Season chicken with salt and pepper, then put in the bowl with the olive oil and mix well so the olive oil evenly coats all of the chicken.
4. Put a few chunks of chicken at a time into the breadcrumb mixture to coat, then on the basket.
5. Lightly spray the top with olive oil spray then air fry 8 minutes, turning halfway. Until golden.

Nutritional Information

- Calories: 188
- Fat: 5g
- Carbs: 8g
- Protein: 25g

Air Fryer Lemon Pepper Chicken

Preparation Time: 15 minutes

Yield: 1 Serving

Ingredients

- 1 Chicken Breast
- 2 Lemons rind and juice
- 1 Tbsp Chicken Seasoning
- 1 Tsp Garlic Puree
- Handful Black Peppercorns
- Salt & Pepper

Directions

1. Preheat the air fryer to 180c.
2. Set up your work station. Place a large sheet of silver foil on the work top and add to it all the seasonings and the lemon rind.
3. Lay out your chicken breasts onto a chopping board and trim off any fatty bits or any little bones that are still there. Then season each side with salt and pepper. Rub the chicken seasoning into both sides so that it is slightly a different colour.
4. Place it in the silver foil sheet and rub it well so that it is fully seasoned.
5. Then seal it up very tight so that it cant breathe as this will help get the flavour into it.
6. Then give it a slap with a rolling pin so that it will flatten it out and release more flavour.
7. Place it in the air fryer for 15 minutes and check to see if it is fully cooked in the middle before serving.
8. Serve.

Nutritional Information

- Calories: 140
- Fat: 2g
- Carbs: 24g
- Protein: 13g

Nashville Hot Chicken

Preparation Time: 45 minutes

Yield: 8 Servings

Ingredients

- 1/2 cup ranch dressing
- 1/4 cup finely chopped dill pickles
- 4 tablespoons butter, melted
- 1 tablespoon ground red pepper (cayenne)
- 1 tablespoon packed dark brown sugar
- 1 teaspoon salt
- 1 teaspoon black pepper
- 1 teaspoon chili powder
- 1 teaspoon garlic powder
- 1 teaspoon smoked paprika
- 2 lb fresh or frozen (thawed) chicken wingettes and drummettes

Directions

1. In small bowl, mix ranch dressing and pickles. Cover and refrigerate sauce until ready to serve.
2. In large bowl, mix melted butter, ground red pepper, brown sugar, salt, pepper, chili powder, garlic powder and smoked paprika.
3. Place chicken in air fryer basket. Set to 350°F; cook 15 minutes, turning and stirring once. Transfer chicken to butter mixture in bowl; toss to coat. Return chicken to air fryer basket. Pour any remaining butter mixture over chicken. Set to 400°F; cook 12 to 15 minutes longer or until juice of chicken is clear when thickest part is cut to bone (at least 165°F), turning and stirring once. Serve with ranch dressing mixture.

Nutritional Information

- Calories: 320
- Fat: 26g
- Carbs: 4g
- Protein: 19g

Henry Wilson

Air-Fried Buttermilk Chicken

Preparation Time: 15 minutes

Yield: 4 Servings

Ingredients

- 800g store-bought chicken thighs (skin on, bone in)

Marinade

- 2 cups buttermilk
- 2 teaspoons salt
- 2 teaspoons black pepper
- 1 teaspoon cayenne pepper

Seasoned flour

- 2 cups all purpose flour
- 1 tablespoon baking powder
- 1 tablespoon garlic powder
- 1 tablespoon paprika powder
- 1 teaspoon salt

Directions

1. Rinse chicken thighs to remove any obvious fat and residue, and pat dry with paper towels.
2. Toss together chicken pieces, black pepper, paprika and salt in a large bowl to coat. Pour buttermilk over until chicken is coated. Refrigerated for at least 6 hours or overnight.
3. Preheat airfryer at 180°C
4. In separate bowl, combine flour, baking powder, paprika and salt and pepper. Remove the chicken 1 piece at a time from the buttermilk and dredge in seasoned flour. Shake off any excess flour and transfer to a plate.
5. Arrange chicken one layer on the fryer basket, skin side up, and slide the basket into the airfryer. Set timer and air fry for 8 minutes. Pull out the tray, turn chicken pieces over, and set timer for another 10 minutes.
6. Allow to drain on paper towels and serve.

Nutritional Information

- Calories: 320
- Fat: 26g
- Carbs: 13g
- Protein: 19g

Copycat KFC Popcorn Chicken

Preparation Time: 15 minutes

Yield: 1 Servings

Ingredients

- 1 Chicken Breast
- 2 ml KFC Spice Blend 60 ml Bread Crumbs
- 1 Small Egg beaten
- 50 g Plain Flour
- Salt & Pepper

Directions

1. In the food processor blend your chicken until it resembles minced chicken.
2. Set up a factory line with a bowl with your flour and a second bowl with your beaten egg. In a third bowl mix together your KFC spice blend, your salt and pepper and then your bread crumbs.
3. Then like a factory line up make your minced chicken into balls and roll in the flour, the egg and then the spiced bread crumbs.
4. Place in the airfryer at 180c for 10-12 minutes or until cooked in the middle.

Nutritional Information

- Calories: 44
- Fat: 0g
- Carbs: 3g
- Protein: 2g

Chicken Tikkas

Preparation Time: 15 minutes

Yield: 4 Servings

Ingredients

For marinade-

- Boneless Chicken – 500 gms, cut into bite sized pieces.
- Thick yoghurt – 200 gms
- Bell peppers – 3 (any color of your choice), cut in an inch chunks.
- Cherry Tomatoes – 100 gms
- Fresh ginger garlic paste – 1 tbsp
- Red Chilli Powder – 2 tbsp
- Turmeric Powder – 1 tsp

- Coriander Powder – 2 tbsp
- Cumin Powder – 2 tbsp
- Olive oil – 2 tsp
- Salt to taste
- Garam masala powder – 1 tsp (adjust as per the spice you want)

For Garnishing –

- Fresh Coriander – ⅓ cup, chopped
- Fresh Mint Leaves – few
- Onion – 1, thinly sliced
- Lemon – 1, cut in half

Directions

1. In a large bowl, mix together all the ingredients under marinade and coat the chicken well with spices. Cover and let it sit for 2 hours. If possible, overnight.
2. Ask your children to help you in threading the chicken, tomatoes and peppers alternatively on the skewers and keep them ready.
3. Preheat Air Fryer for 5 minutes at 200 Degrees C.
4. Line the basket with aluminum foil and place the skewers.
5. Grill for 12-15 minutes, turning each skewer once in between so it cooks evenly.
6. Remove in a plate. Garnish with coriander, mint, onions and squeeze a lime before serving.

Nutritional Information

- Calories: 137
- Fat: 3g

- Carbs: 5g
- Protein: 22g

Flourless Chicken Cordon Bleu

Preparation Time: 30 minutes

Yield: 2 Servings

Ingredients

- 2 Chicken Breasts
- 1 Slice Cheddar Cheese
- 1 Tbsp Soft Cheese
- 1 Slice Ham
- 20g Oats
- 1 Small Egg beaten
- 1 Tsp Garlic Puree
- 1 Tsp Parsley
- 1 Tbsp Tarragon
- 1 Tbsp Thyme
- Salt & Pepper

Directions

1. Preheat your air fryer to 180c.
2. On a chopping board place your chicken breasts. Chop them at a side angle to right near to the corner so that you can fold them over and add ingredients to the centre.
3. Sprinkle all sides of your chicken with salt, pepper and tarragon.
4. In a mixing bowl add the soft cheese, garlic and parsley and mix well.
5. Place a layer of the cheese mixture in the middle along with ½ a slice each of the cheddar cheese and the ham.
6. Press down on the chicken so that it looks like it is sealed with a layer of filling inside it.
7. In one bowl add the egg and in another add the blended oats.
8. In the blended oats bowl also add the thyme and mix well.
9. Roll the chicken in the oats first, then the egg and back in the oats.
10. Place your chicken pieces on a baking sheet in your air fryer and cook for 30 minutes at 180c. After 20 minutes turn it over so that both sides have the chance to be crispy.
11. Serve with new potatoes.

Nutritional Information

- Calories: 137
- Fat: 3g
- Carbs: 5g
- Protein: 22g

Air Fryer KFC Chicken Strips

Preparation Time: 15 minutes

Yield: 8 Servings

Ingredients

- 1 Chicken Breast chopped into strips
- 15 ml Desiccated Coconut

- 15 ml Plain Oats
- 5 ml KFC Spice Blend
- 75 ml Bread Crumbs
- 50 g Plain Flour
- 1 Small Egg beaten
- Salt & Pepper

Directions

1. Chop up your chicken breast into strips.
2. In one bowl add your coconut, oats, KFC spice blend, bread crumbs and salt and pepper.
3. In another bowl have your egg and in another your plain flour.
4. Put your strips in the plain flour, then in the egg and finally in the spicy layer.
5. Place in the Air fryer at 180c and cook for 8 minutes and then cook for a further 4 minutes on 160c so that the chicken has plenty of time to cook in the centre.
6. Serve.

Nutritional Information

- Calories: 94
- Fat: 3g
- Carbs: 13g
- Protein: 4g

Pickle-Brined Fried Chicken

Preparation Time: 15 minutes

Yield: 4 Servings

Ingredients

- 4 chicken legs (bone-in and skin-on), cut into drumsticks and thighs (about 3½ pounds)
- pickle juice from a 24-ounce jar of kosher dill pickles

- ½ cup flour
- salt and freshly ground black pepper
- 2 eggs
- 2 tablespoons vegetable or canola oil
- 1 cup fine breadcrumbs
- 1 teaspoon salt
- 1 teaspoon freshly ground black pepper
- ½ teaspoon ground paprika
- ⅛ teaspoon cayenne pepper
- vegetable or canola oil in a spray bottle

Directions

1. Place the chicken in a shallow dish and pour the pickle juice over the top. Cover and transfer the chicken to the refrigerator to brine in the pickle juice for 3 to 8 hours.
2. When you are ready to cook, remove the chicken from the refrigerator to let it come to room temperature while you set up a dredging station. Place the flour in the a shallow dish and season well with salt and freshly ground black pepper. Whisk the eggs and vegetable oil together in a second shallow dish. In a third shallow dish, combine the breadcrumbs, salt, pepper, paprika and cayenne pepper.
3. Pre-heat the air fryer to 370°F.
4. Remove the chicken from pickle brine and gently dry it with a clean kitchen towel. Dredge each piece of chicken in the flour, then dip it into the egg mixture, and finally press it into the breadcrumb mixture to coat all sides of the chicken. Place the breaded chicken on a plate or baking sheet and spray each piece all over with vegetable oil.
5. Air-fry the chicken in two batches. Place two chicken thighs and two drumsticks into the air fryer basket. Air-fry for 10 minutes. Then, gently turn the chicken pieces over and air fry for another 10 minutes. Remove the chicken

pieces and let them rest on plate – do not cover. Repeat with the second batch of chicken, air frying for 20 minutes, turning the chicken over halfway through.
6. Lower the temperature of the air fryer to 340°F. Place the first batch of chicken on top of the second batch already in the basket and air fry for an additional 7 minutes. Serve warm and enjoy.

Nutritional Information

- Calories: 542
- Fat: 36g
- Carbs: 6g
- Protein: 46g

Air Fryer Southern-Style Chicken

Preparation Time: 15 minutes

Yield: 4 Servings

Ingredients

- 2 cups crushed Ritz crackers (about 50)
- 1 tablespoon minced fresh parsley
- 1 teaspoon garlic salt
- 1 teaspoon paprika
- 1/2 teaspoon pepper
- 1/4 teaspoon ground cumin
- 1/4 teaspoon rubbed sage
- 1 large egg, beaten

- 1 broiler/fryer chicken (3 to 4 pounds), cut up

Directions

1. Preheat air fryer to 375°. Spritz the air fryer basket with cooking spray.
2. In a shallow bowl, mix the first seven ingredients. Place egg in a separate shallow bowl. Dip chicken in egg, then in cracker mixture, patting to help coating adhere. Place a few pieces of chicken in a single layer in the prepared basket, spritz with cooking spray.
3. Cook 10 minutes. Turn chicken and spritz with additional cooking spray; cook until chicken is golden brown and juices run clear, 10-20 minutes longer. Repeat with remaining chicken.

Nutritional Information

- Calories: 405
- Fat: 22g
- Carbs: 13g
- Protein: 36g

Air Fryer Ranch Chicken Tenders

Preparation Time: 15 minutes

Yield: 4 Servings

Ingredients

- 8 chicken tenders, raw
- canola or non-fat cooking spray

For the Dredge Station:

- 1 cup panko breadcrumbs
- 1 egg
- 2 tablespoons of water
- For the Ranch Chicken Seasoning:
- 1/2 tsp Salt
- 1/4 tsp Black pepper, more or less to taste
- 1/2 tsp Garlic powder
- 1/2 tsp Onion powder
- 1/4 tsp Paprika
- 1 tsp Dried parsley

Directions

1. Preheat the Air Fryer. Warm the air fryer by setting it to 400 degrees F for 5 minutes. Allow it to run without any food in the basket.
2. Set up a dredging station. Whisk the water and egg together in a shallow bowl. Pour the Panko Breadcrumbs in another shallow bowl.
3. Prepare the Ranch Seasoning. In a small bowl, combine all the seasonings for the ranch seasoning.
4. Season the Chicken. Sprinkle the chicken tenders with the ranch seasoning, turning to coat both sides.
5. Dredge the chicken. Dip chicken tenders into the egg wash and then press it into the panko. Turn to coat both sides.
6. Load the Fryer Basket. Place the breaded tenders into the fry basket. Repeat with remaining tenders. You may need to fry in batches.
7. Fry the Chicken. Place the Fry Basket into the Power Air Fryer XL. Spray a light coat of canola oil of non-fat cooking spray over the panko. Press the M button. Scroll to the Fried Chicken Icon (400 degrees F). Press the Power Button. Adjust the cooking time to 12 minutes at

400 degrees. Halfway through cooking, flip the tenders over to brown the other side. The tenders are done when the center of the fattest part of the tender is 165 degrees F, the flesh is no longer pink, and the juices run clear.

Nutritional Information

- Calories: 197
- Fat: 4g
- Carbs: 12g
- Protein: 25g

6. Meat Recipes

Stromboli

Preparation Time: 15 minutes

Yield: 4 Servings

Ingredients

- 12 ounce pizza crust, refrigerated
- 3 cup cheddar cheese, shredded
- 0.75 cup Mozzarella cheese, shredded
- 1/2 pound cooked ham, sliced
- 3 ounce red bell peppers, roasted
- 1 egg yolk
- 1 tablespoon milk

Directions

1. Roll the dough out until 1/4 inch thick.
2. Layer the ham, cheese and peppers on one side of the dough. Fold over to seal.
3. Mix the egg and milk together and brush the dough.
4. Place the stromboli into the Fry Basket and place it into the Power Air Fryer XL.
5. Press the M Button. Scroll to the Chicken icon.
6. Press the Power Button & adjust cooking time to 15 minutes at 360 degrees.
7. Every 5 minutes, carefully turn stromboli over.

Nutritional Information

- Calories: 329
- Fat: 12g
- Carbs: 34g
- Protein: 18g

Henry Wilson

Roasted Stuffed Peppers

Preparation Time: 15 minutes

Yield: 4 Servings

Ingredients

- 2 medium green peppers, stems and seeds removed - cooked in boiling salted water for 3 minutes
- ½ medium onion, chopped

- 1 clove garlic, minced
- 1 teaspoon olive oil
- 8 ounces lean ground beef
- ½ cup tomato sauce
- 1 teaspoon Worcestershire sauce
- ½ teaspoon salt
- ½ teaspoon black pepper
- 4 ounces cheddar cheese, shredded

Directions

1. Preheat air fryer to 390 setting.
2. Sauté the onion and garlic in the olive oil in a small nonstick skillet until golden and remove from burner to cool. Blend the beef, cooked vegetables, ¼ cup tomato sauce, Worcestershire, salt and pepper and half the shredded cheese in a medium bowl. Divide and stuff the pepper halves - top with remaining tomato sauce and cheese.
3. Arrange in the air fryer basket and air fry or bake until meat is cooked through - 15 to 20 minutes.

Nutritional Information

- Calories: 311
- Fat: 9g
- Carbs: 31g
- Protein: 25g

Air Fryer Beef Empanadas

Preparation Time: 15 minutes

Yield: 4 Servings

Ingredients

- 8 Goya empanada discs, thawed
- 1 cup picadillo
- 1 egg white, whisked
- 1 teaspoon water

Directions

1. Preheat the air fryer to 325F for 8 minutes. Spray the basket generously with cooking spray.
2. Place 2 tbsp of picadillo in the center of each disc. Fold in half and use a fork to seal the edges. Repeat with the remaining dough.
3. Whisk the egg whites with water, then brush the tops of the empanadas.
4. Bake 2 or 3 at a time in the air fryer 8 minutes, or until golden. Remove from heat and repeat with the remaining empanadas.

Nutritional Information

- Calories: 183
- Fat: 5g
- Carbs: 22g
- Protein: 11g

Air-Fried Turkey Breast with Maple Mustard Glaze

Preparation Time: 35 minutes

Yield: 4 Servings

Ingredients

- 2 teaspoons olive oil
- 5-pound whole turkey breast
- 1 teaspoon dried thyme
- ½ teaspoon dried sage
- ½ teaspoon smoked paprika
- 1 teaspoon salt
- ½ teaspoon freshly ground black pepper
- ¼ cup maple syrup
- 2 tablespoon Dijon mustard
- 1 tablespoon butter

Directions

1. Pre heat air fryer to 350°F.
2. Brush the olive oil all over the turkey breast.
3. Combine the thyme, sage, paprika, salt and pepper and rub the outside of the turkey breast with the spice mixture.
4. Transfer the seasoned turkey breast to the air fryer basket and air-fry at 350°F for 25 minutes. Turn the turkey breast on its side and air-fry for another 12 minutes. Turn the turkey breast on the opposite side and air-fry for another 12 minutes. The internal temperature of the turkey breast should reach 165°F when fully cooked.
5. While the turkey is air-frying, combine the maple syrup, mustard and butter in a small saucepan. When the cooking time is up, return the turkey breast to an upright position and brush the glaze all over the turkey. Air-fry for a final 5 minutes, until the skin is nicely browned and crispy. Let the turkey rest, loosely tented with foil, for at least 5 minutes before slicing and serving.

Nutritional Information

- Calories: 183
- Fat: 5g
- Carbs: 22g
- Protein: 11g

Henry Wilson

Crispy Boneless Breaded Pork Chops

Preparation Time: 15 minutes

Yield: 4 Servings

Ingredients

- 6 (3/4-inch thick) center cut boneless pork chops, fat trimmed (5 oz each)

- kosher salt
- 1 large egg, beaten
- 1/2 cup panko crumbs
- 1/3 cup crushed cornflakes crumbs
- 2 tbsp grated parmesan cheese (omit for vegetarian)
- 1 1/4 tsp sweet paprika
- 1/2 tsp garlic powder
- 1/2 tsp onion powder
- 1/4 tsp chili powder
- 1/8 tsp black pepper

Directions

1. Preheat the air fryer to 400F for 12 minutes and lightly spray the basket with oil.
2. Season pork chops on both sides with 1/2 tsp kosher salt.
3. Combine panko, cornflake crumbs, parmesan cheese, 3/4 tsp kosher salt, paprika, garlic powder, onion powder, chili powder and black pepper in a large shallow bowl.
4. Place the beaten egg in another. Dip the pork into the egg, then crumb mixture.
5. When the air fryer is ready, place 3 of the chops into the prepared basket and spritz the top with oil.
6. Cook 12 minutes turning half way, spritzing both sides with oil. Set aside and repeat with the remaining.

Nutritional Information

- Calories: 378
- Fat: 13g
- Carbs: 8g
- Protein: 33g

Turkey Breast with Cherry Glaze

Preparation Time: 15 minutes

Yield: 4 Servings

Ingredients

- 1 (5-pound) turkey breast
- 2 teaspoons olive oil
- 1 teaspoon dried thyme
- ½ teaspoon dried sage
- 1 teaspoon salt
- ½ teaspoon freshly ground black pepper
- ½ cup cherry preserve
- 1 tablespoon chopped fresh thyme leaves
- 1 teaspoon soy sauce
- freshly ground black pepper

Directions

1. Pre-heat the air fryer to 350°F.
2. Brush the turkey breast all over with the olive oil. Combine the thyme, sage, salt and pepper and rub the outside of the turkey breast with the spice mixture.
3. Transfer the seasoned turkey breast to the air fryer basket, breast side up, and air-fry at 350°F for 25 minutes. Turn the turkey breast on its side and air-fry for another 12 minutes. Turn the turkey breast on the opposite side and air-fry for another 12 minutes. The internal temperature of the turkey breast should reach 165°F when fully cooked.
4. While the turkey is air-frying, combine the cherry preserve, fresh thyme, soy sauce and pepper in a small bowl. When the cooking time is up, return the turkey breast to an upright position and brush the glaze all over the turkey. Air-fry for a final 5 minutes, until the skin is nicely browned and crispy. Let the turkey rest before serving.

Nutritional Information

- Calories: 167
- Fat: 6g
- Carbs: 1g
- Protein: 25g

Air Fryer Coffee & Spice Ribeye

Preparation Time: 15 minutes

Yield: 4 Servings

Ingredients

- 1 lb. ribeye steak
- 1 1/2 tsp. course sea salt
- 1 tsp. brown sugar
- 1/2 tsp. ground coffee
- 1/2 tsp. black pepper
- 1/4 tsp. chili powder
- 1/4 tsp. garlic powder
- 1/4 tsp. onion powder
- 1/4 tsp. paprika
- 1/4 tsp. chipotle powder

- 1/8 tsp. coriander
- 1/8 tsp. cocoa powder

Directions

1. In a small bowl – add all spices. Using a whisk – combine spices, making sure to break up the brown sugar.
2. Sprinkle a generous amount of spice mix onto a plate. Lay one steak on top of spices. Then season steak liberally with spice mix and rub into meat evenly. Flip to make sure other side is seasoned properly as well.
3. Pick up steak and press all sides into remaining spice mix on the plate so that none of the spices are wasted.
4. Let steak sit for at least 20 minutes to come to room temperature. This helps the steak to cook evenly.
5. Meanwhile - Prepare the air fryer tray by coating with oil to prevent sticking. Preheat air fryer to 390 degrees for at least 3 minutes.
6. Cook steak undisturbed for 9 minutes. Do not flip and do not open.
7. Once cooking time is finished, remove from air fryer and let rest for at least 5 minutes before slicing.

Nutritional Information

- Calories: 495
- Fat: 32g
- Carbs: 5g
- Protein: 46g

Air Fried Meatloaf

Preparation Time: 25 minutes

Yield: 4 Servings

Ingredients

- 1 pound lean ground beef
- 1 egg, lightly beaten
- 3 tablespoons dry bread crumbs
- 1 small onion, finely chopped
- 1 tablespoon chopped fresh thyme
- 1 teaspoon saltground black pepper to taste
- 2 mushrooms, thickly sliced
- 1 tablespoon olive oil, or as needed

Directions

1. Preheat an air fryer to 392 degrees F (200 degrees C).
2. Combine ground beef, egg, bread crumbs, onion, thyme, salt, and pepper in a bowl. Knead and mix thoroughly.
3. Transfer beef mixture to a baking pan and smooth the top. Press mushrooms into the top and coat with olive oil. Place the pan into the air fryer basket and slide into the air fryer.
4. Set air fryer timer for 25 minutes and roast meatloaf until nicely browned.
5. Let meatloaf rest at least 10 minutes before slicing into wedges and serving.

Nutritional Information

- Calories: 297
- Fat: 19g
- Carbs: 6g
- Protein: 24g

Air Fryer Chinese Salt and Pepper Pork Chops

Preparation Time: 15 minutes

Yield: 2 Servings

Ingredients

Pork Chops:
- 1 Egg White
- 1/2 teaspoon Sea Salt

- 1/4 teaspoon Freshly Ground Black Pepper
- 3/4 cup Potato Starch (or cornstarch)
- 1 Oil Mister

Str Fry:

- 2 Jalapeño Pepper stems removed, sliced
- 2 Scallions (Green Onions) trimmes, sliced
- 2 Tablespoons Canola Oil (or peanut)
- 1 teaspoon Sea Salt
- 1/4 teaspoon Freshly Ground Black Pepper
- Cast Iron Chicken Fryer

Directions

1. Coat Air Fryer Basket with a thin coat of Oil. In a medium bowl, whisk together egg white, salt and pepper until foamy. Slice pork chops into cutlet pieces, leaving a little on the bones and pat dry. Add pork chop pieces to egg white mixture. Coat thoroughly. Marinate for at least 20 minutes.
2. Transfer pork chops into a large bowl and add Potato Starch. Dredge the pork chops through the Potato Starch thoroughly. Shake off pork and place into a prepared Air Fryer Basket. Lightly spray pork with oil.
3. Cook at 360 degrees for 9 minutes, shaking the basket often and spraying with oil between shakes. Cook an additional 6 minutes at 400 degrees, or until the pork is brown and crispy.

Stir Fry:

4. Slice Jalapeños thin and remove seeds. Chop scallions. Place in bowl and set aside.
5. Heat wok or skillet until screaming hot. Add oil, Jalapeño peppers, Scallions, salt and pepper and stir fry for about a

minute. Add air fried pork pieces to the wok or skillet and toss them with the Jalapeño and Scallions. Stir Fry pork for another minute, making sure they become coated with the hot oil and vegetables.

Nutritional Information

- Calories: 305
- Fat: 13g
- Carbs: 1g
- Protein: 24g

Air Fryer Country Fried Steak

Preparation Time: 15 minutes

Yield: 4 Servings

Ingredients

- 6 ounce sirloin steak-pounded thin
- 3 eggs, beaten
- 1 cup flour
- 1 cup Panko
- 1 teaspoon onion powder
- 1 teaspoon garlic powder
- 1 teaspoon salt
- 1 teaspoon pepper

- 6 ounce ground sausage meat
- 2 tablespoon flour
- 2 cup milk
- 1 teaspoon pepper

Directions

1. Season the panko with the spices
2. Dredge the steak in this order: flour, egg, and seasoned panko
3. Place the breaded steak into the basket of the Air Fryer and close. Press the M button the Defaut temperature of 370 F and set the time for 12 minutes. Press the power button
4. Once the timer has elapsed remove the steak and serve with mash potatoes and sausage gravy.

Sausage Gravy:

5. In a pan cook the sausage until well done. Drain fat, reserve 2 tbsp in the pan.
6. Add in the flour to the pan with sausage, mix until all the flour is incorporated
7. Slowly mix in the milk. Stir over a med heat until the milk thickens
8. Season with pepper. Cook for 3 minutes to cook out the flour.

Nutritional Information

- Calories: 311
- Fat: 15g
- Carbs: 15g
- Protein: 25g

Air Fryer Italian-Style Meatballs

Preparation Time: 45 minutes

Yield: 12 Servings

Ingredients

- 2 tablespoons olive oil
- 1 medium shallot, minced (about 2 Tbsp.)
- 3 cloves garlic, minced (about 1 Tbsp.)
- 1/4 cup whole-wheat panko crumbs
- 2 tablespoons whole milk
- 2/3 pound lean ground beef
- 1/3 pound bulk turkey sausage
- 1 large egg, lightly beaten
- 1/4 cup finely chopped fresh flat-leaf parsley
- 1 tablespoon finely chopped fresh rosemary
- 1 tablespoon finely chopped fresh thyme
- 1 tablespoon Dijon mustard
- 1/2 teaspoon kosher salt

Directions

1. Preheat air-fryer to 400°F. Heat oil in a medium nonstick pan over medium-high heat. Add shallot and cook until softened, 1 to 2 minutes. Add garlic and cook just until fragrant, 1 minute. Remove from heat.
2. In a large bowl, combine panko and milk. Let stand 5 minutes.
3. Add cooked shallot and garlic to panko mixture, along with beef, turkey sausage egg, parsley, rosemary, thyme, mustard, and salt. Stir to gently combine.
4. Gently shape mixture into 1 1/2-inch balls. Place shaped balls in a single-layer in air-fryer basket. Cook half the meatballs at 400°F until lightly browned and cooked-through, 10 to 11 minutes. Remove and keep warm. Repeat with remaining meatballs.
5. Serve warm meatballs with toothpicks as an appetizer or serve over pasta, rice, or spiralized zoodles for a main dish.

Nutritional Information

- Calories: 122
- Fat: 8g
- Carbs: 0g
- Protein: 10g

Air Fried Pork Chops With Brussels Sprouts

Preparation Time: 25 minutes

Yield: 2 Servings

Ingredients

- 8 ounces bone-in center-cut pork chop
- Cooking spray
- 1/8 teaspoon kosher salt
- 1/2 teaspoon black pepper, divided
- 1 teaspoon olive oil
- 1 teaspoon pure maple syrup
- 1 teaspoon Dijon mustard

- 6 ounces Brussels sprouts, quartered

Directions

1. Lightly coat pork chop with cooking spray; sprinkle with salt and 1/4 teaspoon of the pepper. Whisk together oil, syrup, mustard, and remaining 1/4 teaspoon pepper in a medium bowl; add Brussels sprouts; toss to coat.
2. Place pork chop on 1 side of air fryer basket, and coated Brussels sprouts on other side. Heat air fryer to 400°F, and cook until golden brown and pork is cooked to desired temperature, about 10 minutes for medium or 13 minutes for well-done.

Nutritional Information

- Calories: 377
- Fat: 11g
- Carbs: 21g
- Protein: 40g

Thanksgiving Turkey

Preparation Time: 35 minutes

Yield: 4 Servings

Ingredients

- 1 (2-lb.) turkey breast
- Kosher salt
- Freshly ground black pepper
- 1 tsp. freshly chopped thyme
- 1 tsp. freshly chopped rosemary
- 1 tsp. freshly chopped sage
- 1/4 c. maple syrup
- 2 tbsp. dijon mustard

- 1 tbsp. butter, melted

Directions

1. Season turkey breast generously with salt and pepper, then rub all over with fresh herbs.
2. Place in air fryer and fry at 390° for 30 to 35 minutes or until the internal temperature reaches 160°.
3. In a small bowl, whisk together maple syrup, dijon, and melted butter.
4. Remove turkey from air fryer and brush mixture all over. Return to air fryer and fry at 330° until caramelized, 2 minutes.
5. Let rest 15 minutes before slicing.

Nutritional Information

- Calories: 167
- Fat: 7g
- Carbs: 1g
- Protein: 25g

Ultimate Air Fryer Burgers

Preparation Time: 45 minutes

Yield: 4 Servings

Ingredients

- 300 g Mixed Mince pork and beef
- Onion
- 1 Tsp Garlic Puree
- 1 Tsp Tomato Puree
- 1 Tsp Mustard
- 1 Tsp Basil
- 1 Tsp Mixed Herbs
- Salt & Pepper
- 25 g Cheddar Cheese
- 4 Bread Buns

- Salad for burger topping

Directions

1. In a mixing bowl add the mince and seasoning and mix well.
2. Form into four medium sized burgers and place in the Air Fryer cooking tray.
3. Cook in the Air Fryer on 200c for 25 minutes and then check on them and then cook them for further 20 minutes on 180c.
4. Then add your salad, cheese and bun and serve!

Nutritional Information

- Calories: 344
- Fat: 19g
- Carbs: 22g
- Protein: 19g

Perfect Air Fryer Steak with Garlic Herb Butter

Preparation Time: 15 minutes

Yield: 2 Servings

Ingredients

- 2 - 8 oz Ribeye steak
- salt
- freshly cracked black pepper
- olive oil
- Garlic Butter
- 1 stick unsalted butter softened
- 2 Tbsp fresh parsley chopped

- 2 tsp garlic minced
- 1 tsp Worcestershire Sauce
- 1/2 tsp salt

Directions

1. Prepare Garlic Butter by mixing butter, parsley garlic, worcestershire sauce, and salt until thoroughly combined.
2. Place in parchment paper and roll into a log. Refrigerate until ready to use.
3. Remove steak from fridge and allow to sit at room temperature for 20 minutes. Rub a little bit of olive oil on both side of the steak and season with salt and freshly cracked black pepper.
4. Grease your Air Fryer basket by rubbing a little bit of oil on the basket. Preheat Air Fryer to 400 degrees Fahrenheit. Once preheated, place steaks in air fryer and cook for 12 minutes, flipping halfway through.
5. Remove from air fryer and allow to rest for 5 minutes. Top with garlic butter.

Nutritional Information

- Calories: 683
- Fat: 24g
- Carbs: 22g
- Protein: 25g

Air Fryer Mongolian Beef

Preparation Time: 25 minutes

Yield: 4 Servings

Ingredients

Meat

- 1 Lb Flank Steak
- 1/4 Cup Corn Starch

Sauce

- 2 Tsp Vegetable Oil
- 1/2 Tsp Ginger
- 1 Tbsp Minced Garlic
- 1/2 Cup Soy Sauce or Gluten Free Soy Sauce

- 1/2 Cup Water
- 3/4 Cup Brown Sugar Packed

Directions

1. Thinly slice the steak in long pieces, then coat with the corn starch.
2. Place in the Air Fryer and cook on 390 for 10 minutes on each side.
3. While the steak cooks, warm up all sauce ingredient in a medium sized saucepan on medium-high heat.
4. Whisk the ingredients together until it gets to a low boil.
5. Once both the steak and sauce are cooked, place the steak in a bowl with the sauce and let it soak in for about 5-10 minutes.
6. When ready to serve, use tongs to remove the steak and let the excess sauce drip off.
7. Place steak on cooked rice and green beans, top with additional sauce if you prefer.

Nutritional Information

- Calories: 258
- Fat: 11g
- Carbs: 8g
- Protein: 30g

Air Fryer Beef Stir Fry With Homemade Marinade

Preparation Time: 15 minutes

Yield: 4 Servings

Ingredients

- 1 pound of beef sirloin, cut into 2 inch strips
- 1½ pounds of broccoli florets
- 1 red pepper, cut into strips
- 1 green pepper, cut into strips
- 1 yellow pepper, cut into strips
- ½ cup of onion, cut into strips
- ½ cup of red onion, cut into strips

Sauce/Marinade:

- ¼ cup of hoisin sauce
- 2 teaspoons of minced garlic
- 1 teaspoon of sesame oil
- 1 tablespoon of soy sauce
- 1 teaspoon of ground ginger
- ¼ cup of water

Directions

1. Add all of the ingredients for the sauce (marinate) to a bowl, then add the meat.
2. Then place in the refrigerator for about 20 minutes.
3. Add one tablespoon of stir fryer oil, and mix it in with the vegetables.
4. Place your vegetables in the air fryer basket, and cook them for about 5 minutes on 200 degrees F.
5. Then open your air fryer, mix all of the vegetables, and make sure they are softened, not hard. If they aren't softened, add another 2 minutes.
6. Remove the vegetables and place them in a bowl, then add your meat to the air fryer basket, and cook them for 4 minutes at 360. Check and flip them, and do another 2 minutes if they aren't done.
7. I served my stir fry over white rice. Then topped it with the vegetables and meat.

Nutritional Information

- Calories: 160
- Fat: 6g
- Carbs: 0g
- Protein: 25g

Best Air Fryer Cookbook for Beginners

Air Fryer Marinated Steak

Preparation Time: 25 minutes

Yield: 2 Servings

Ingredients

- About 6-8 oz Strip Steaks
- 1 tablespoon low-sodium soy sauce
- 1 teaspoon liquid smoke or a cap full

- 1 tablespoon McCormick's Grill Mates Montreal Steak Seasoning or Steak Rub (or season to taste)
- 1/2 tablespoon unsweetened cocoa powder
- salt and pepper to taste
- melted butter (optional)

Directions

1. Drizzle the Steak with the soy sauce and liquid smoke. You can do this inside Ziploc bags.
2. Season the steak with the seasonings.
3. Refrigerate for at least a couple of hours, preferably overnight.
4. Place the steak in the air fryer. I did not use any oil. Cook two steaks at a time (if air fryer is standard size). You can use an accessory grill pan, a layer rack or the standard air fryer basket.
5. Cook for 5 minutes on 375 degrees. After 5 minutes, open the air fryer and examine your steak. Cook time will vary depending on your desired doneness. Check the inside of the steak to determine if they have finished cooking. You can stick a knife or fork in the center to review the level of pink. You can also use a meat thermometer and cook to 125° F for rare, 135° F for medium-rare, 145° F for medium, 155° F for medium-well, and 160° F for well done.
6. For medium steak, at 5 minutes, I flipped my steak and cooked for an additional 2 minutes, 7 minutes cook time total using the Power Air Fryer. Each air fryer brand is different and will cook at different speeds. I also have the Black + Decker Air Fryer and 5 minutes at 370 degrees was enough time to produce medium done steak. At 7 minutes, the steak was near well done. Examine your steak and do what works best for you.

7. Remove the steak from the air fryer and drizzle with melted butter.

Nutritional Information

- Calories: 476
- Fat: 28g
- Carbs: 1g
- Protein: 49g

Air Fryer Paleo Sirloin Steak

Preparation Time: 25 minutes

Yield: 4 Servings

Ingredients

- 2 Sirloin Steaks
- 2 Tbsp. Primal Palate Steak Seasoning
- Cooking Fat (ghee, coconut oil or avocado oil)

Directions

1. Preheat your air fryer for 5 minutes at 392 degrees

2. Remove the steak from the fridge and pat dry (preferably let it sit out until it is room temperature).
3. Brush (or spray) the top of the sirloin with cooking fat (about 1-2 tsp.) and season generously.
4. Coat the bottom of the air fryer basket in cooking fat and add the sirloin steak to the basket.
5. Cook for 5 minutes.
6. Flip the sirloin steak and cook an additional 5 minutes.
7. Remove the steak from the air fryer and let it rest for 5 minutes before slicing and servings.

Nutritional Information

- Calories: 276
- Fat: 15g
- Carbs: 5g
- Protein: 25g

Air Fryer Steak Fajita's

Preparation Time: 25 minutes

Yield: 4 Servings

Ingredients

- 1.25 lbs. of Beef Steak Strips Stir Fry Cut
- 1 Red Bell Pepper julienned
- 1 Yellow Bell Pepper julienned
- 1 Green Bell Pepper julienned
- 1 Red Onion sliced
- 2 teaspoon of Garlic Powder
- 1 teaspoon of Paprika
- 1 teaspoon of Chili Powder

- 2 teaspoon of ground Cumin
- 1 teaspoon of Mexican Oregano
- 1 teaspoon of Salt
- 2 tablespoon of Salt

Directions

1. In a small bowl, combine the garlic powder, paprika, chili powder, cumin, oregano and salt. Mix it well.
2. In a large bowl, combine the julienned peppers, sliced onion and the beef strips.
3. Place the prepared spice blend in with the oil. Give everything a good mix, making sure the beef and the peppers are well coated in oil and the spice blend.
4. Divide the mix into two batches.
5. Spread one batch of the beef and vegetables in a well-greased air fryer basket.
6. Air fry at 390 F for 10 minutes.
7. Repeat with the other batch.
8. Serve hot in a warmed white or yellow corn tortilla and your favorite add-ins and a squeeze of lime juice.

Nutritional Information

- Calories: 329
- Fat: 18g
- Carbs: 5g
- Protein: 32g

7. Vegetable Recipes

Air Fryer Fried Ravioli

Preparation Time: 10 minutes

Yield: 6 Servings

Ingredients

- 1 (14-ounce) jar marinara sauce

- 1 (9-ounce) box cheese ravioli, store-bought or meat ravioli
- 1 teaspoon olive oil
- 2 cups Italian-style bread crumbs
- 1 cup buttermilk
- 1/4 cup Parmesan cheese

Directions

1. Dip ravioli in buttermilk. Add olive oil to breadcrumbs, then press the ravioli into it.
2. Put breaded ravioli into heated airfryer on baking paper and cook at 200°F for about 5 minutes.
3. Serve warm with marinara sauce for dipping.

Nutritional Information

- Calories: 319
- Fat: 12g
- Carbs: 52g
- Protein: 17g

Spicy Cauliflower Stir-Fry

Preparation Time: 30 minutes

Yield: 4 Servings

Ingredients

- 1 head cauliflower cut into florets
- 3/4 cup onion white, thinly sliced
- 5 cloves garlic finely sliced

- 1 1/2 tablespoons tamari or gluten free tamari
- 1 tablespoon rice vinegar
- 1/2 teaspoon coconut sugar
- 1 tablespoon Sriracha or other favorite hot sauce
- 2 scallions for garnish

Directions

1. Place cauliflower in the air fryer. If your air fryer is one that has holes in the bottom you'll need to use an air fryer insert.
2. Set the temp to 350 degrees. Cook 10 minutes.
3. Open the air fryer, grab the pot by the handle, remove and shake and slide back in the compartment.
4. Add the sliced onion, stir and cook 10 more minutes.
5. Add garlic, stir and cook 5 more minutes.
6. Mix soy sauce, rice vinegar, coconut sugar, Sriracha, salt & pepper together in a small bowl.
7. Add the mixture to cauliflower and stir. Cook 5 more minutes. The insert keeps all of the juices inside.
8. To serve sprinkle sliced scallions over the top for garnish.

Nutritional Information

- Calories: 93
- Fat: 3g
- Carbs: 12g
- Protein: 4g

Henry Wilson

Air Fried Cauliflower Rice

Preparation Time: 20 minutes

Yield: 3 Servings

Ingredients

Round 1

- 1/2 block firm or extra firm tofu
- 2 tablespoons reduced sodium soy sauce
- 1/2 cup diced onion
- 1 cup diced carrot - about 1 1/2 to 2 carrots
- 1 teaspoon turmeric

Round 2

- 3 cups riced cauliflower - Cauliflower minced into pieces smaller than the size of a pea. You can do this by hand with a box-style cheese crater, use your food processor to pulse into pieces, or buy pre-riced, bagged cauliflower.
- 2 tablespoons reduced sodium soy sauce
- 1 1/2 teaspoons toasted sesame oil - optional, but recommended
- 1 tablespoon rice vinegar
- 1 tablespoon minced ginger
- 1/2 cup finely chopped broccoli
- 2 cloves garlic - minced
- 1/2 cup frozen peas

Directions

1. In a large bowl, crumble the tofu (you're going for scrambled egg-size pieces, not ricotta here), then toss with the rest of the Round 1 ingredients. Air fry at 370F for 10 minutes, shaking once.
2. Meanwhile, toss together all of the Round 2 ingredients in a large bowl.
3. When that first 10 minutes of cooking are done, add all of the Round 2 ingredients to your air fryer, shake gently, and fry at 370 for 10 more minutes, shaking after 5 minutes.
4. Riced cauliflower can vary quite a bit in size, so if you feel like yours doesn't look done enough at this point, you can

cook for an additional 2-5 minutes at 370F. Just shake and check in every couple of minutes until it's done to your liking.

Nutritional Information

- Calories: 153
- Fat: 3g
- Carbs: 12g
- Protein: 10g

Air Fried Sticky Mushroom Rice

Preparation Time: 20 minutes

Yield: 6 Servings

Ingredients

- 16 ounces jasmine rice uncooked
- 1/2 cup soy sauce you can use gluten free tamari
- 4 tablespoons maple syrup

- 4 cloves garlic finely chopped
- 2 teaspoon Chinese 5 Spice
- 1/2 teaspoon ground ginger
- 4 tablespoons white wine you can use rice vinegar
- 16 ounces cremini mushrooms wiped clean, you can cut any huge mushrooms in half
- 1/2 cup peas frozen

Directions

1. Start your rice now so that it will be done and hot at the same time as the sauce.
2. Mix the next 6 ingredients together and set aside.
3. Place the mushrooms in the air fryer. If you can set your degrees - set it to 350 degrees. Otherwise just turn it on. My Air Fryer temp is built in and always cooks at 338 degrees. Cook for 10 minutes.
4. Open the air fryer, if you don't have one that stirs itself, pull out the pot and shake.
5. Pour the liquid mixture and peas over the top of the mushrooms. Stir and cook 5 more minutes.
6. Pour the mushroom/pea sauce over the pot of rice and stir. Serve.

Nutritional Information

- Calories: 366
- Fat: 1g
- Carbs: 77g
- Protein: 10g

Air-Fried Asparagus

Preparation Time: 20 minutes

Yield: 2 Servings

Ingredients

- 1/2 bunch of asparagus, with bottom 2 inches trimmed off
- Avocado or Olive Oil in an oil mister or sprayer
- 1 tsp. Himalayan salt
- 1/ tsp Black pepper

Directions

1. Place trimmed asparagus spears in the air-fryer basket. Spritz spears lightly with oil, then sprinkle with salt and a tiny bit of black pepper.
2. Place basket inside air-fryer and bake at 400° for 10 minutes.
3. Serve immediately.

Nutritional Information

- Calories: 118
- Fat: 8g
- Carbs: 10g
- Protein: 5g

Air Fried Zucchini, Yellow Squash, and Carrots

Preparation Time: 20 minutes

Yield: 2 Servings

Ingredients

- ½ pound carrots, peeled and cut into 1-inch cubes
- 6 teaspoons olive oil

- 1 pound zucchini, stem and root ends trimmed and cut into ¾-inch half moons
- 1 pound yellow squash, stem and root ends trimmed and cut into ¾-inch half moons
- 1 teaspoon kosher salt
- ½ teaspoon ground white pepper
- 1 tablespoon tarragon leaves, roughly chopped

Directions

1. In a small bowl, combine the carrot cubes with 2 teaspoons of the olive oil and toss well to combine. Place the carrots in the basket of the Air Fryer and close the drawer. Set the temperature to 400 degrees Fahrenheit and the timer to 5 minutes.
2. While the carrots cook, place the zucchini and yellow squash pieces in a medium bowl. Drizzle with the remaining 4 teaspoons of olive oil and season with the salt and pepper. Toss well to coat the vegetables evenly. Once the timer goes off, add the zucchini and yellow squash to the basket of the Air Fryer along with the carrots and close the drawer. Set the timer for 30 minutes and cook the vegetables, tossing two or three times throughout the cooking process to ensure even browning.
3. When the timer goes off, remove the vegetables from the Air Fryer and toss with the tarragon. Serve warm.

Nutritional Information

- Calories: 118
- Fat: 8g
- Carbs: 10g
- Protein: 5g

Healthy Mediterranean Vegetables

Preparation Time: 20 minutes

Yield: Servings

Ingredients

- 50 g Cherry Tomatoes
- 1 Large Courgette
- 1 Green Pepper
- 1 Large Parsnip
- 1 Medium Carrot
- 1 Tsp Mixed Herbs
- 2 Tbsp Honey
- 1 Tsp Mustard
- 2 Tsp Garlic Puree
- 6 Tbsp Olive Oil

- Salt & Pepper

Directions

1. In the bottom of your Airfryer (chopping as you go) slice up the courgette and green pepper. Peel and dice the parsnip and carrot and add the cherry tomatoes whole while still on the vine for extra flavour.
2. Drizzle with three tablespoons of olive oil and cook for 15 minutes at 180c.
3. In the meantime mix up the rest of your ingredients into an Air fryer safe baking dish.
4. When the vegetables are done transfer them from the bottom of the Airfryer into the baking dish and shake well so that all the vegetables are covered in the marinade.
5. Sprinkle with a little more salt and pepper and cook for 5 minutes on 200c.
6. Serve.

Nutritional Information

- Calories: 280
- Fat: 21g
- Carbs: 21g
- Protein: 2g

Lemony Green Beans

Preparation Time: 10 minutes

Yield: 2 Servings

Ingredients

- 1 lb. green beans, washed and destemmed
- 1 lemon
- Pinch of salt

- Black pepper to taste
- 1/4 teaspoon oil

Directions

1. Put green beans in air fryer.
2. Add a few squeezes of lemon.
3. Add salt and pepper.
4. Drizzle oil over top.
5. Cook in Air Fryer at 400 degrees for 10-12 minutes.

Nutritional Information

- Calories: 52
- Fat: 3g
- Carbs: 5g
- Protein: 1g

Crispy Roasted Broccoli

Preparation Time: 10 minutes

Yield: 2 Servings

Ingredients

- 2 tbsps yogurt
- 1 tbsp chickpea flour
- 1/4 tsp turmeric powder
- 1/2 tsp salt

- 1/2 tsp red chilli powder
- 1/4 tsp masala chat

Directions

1. To prepare crispy roasted broccoli, we need to cut the broccoli into small florets. Soak in a bowl of water with 2 tsp salt for 30 minutes to remove any impurities or worms.
2. Remove the broccoli florets from the water. Drain well and wipe thoroughly using a kitchen towel to absorb all the moisture.
3. In a bowl, mix together all the ingredients for the marinade.
4. Toss the broccoli florets in this marinade. Cover and keep aside in the refrigerator for 15 minutes.
5. When the broccoli is marinated, preheat the airfryer at 200°C. Open the basket of the airfryer and place the marinated florets inside. Push the basket back in, and turn the time dial to 10 minutes.
6. Give the basket a shake once midway and then check after 10 minutes if golden and crisp. If not, keep for another 2-3 minutes. Eat them hot!
7. If you don't have an air fryer, use a preheated oven and spread the florets on a lined baking tray and bake for around 15 minutes in a preheated oven at 190°C or until golden and crisp.

Nutritional Information

- Calories: 96
- Fat: 1g
- Carbs: 15g

- Protein: 7g

Henry Wilson

Roasted Rainbow Vegetables

Preparation Time: 20 minutes

Yield: 4 Servings

Ingredients

- 1 red bell pepper, seeded and cut into 1-inch pieces
- 1 yellow summer squash, cut into 1-inch pieces
- 1 zucchini, cut into 1-inch pieces
- 4 ounces fresh mushrooms, cleaned and halved
- 1/2 sweet onion, cut into 1-inch wedges
- 1 tablespoon extra-virgin olive oil
- salt and pepper to taste

Directions

1. Preheat an air fryer according to manufacturer's recommendations.
2. Place red bell pepper, summer squash, zucchini, mushrooms, and onion in a large bow. Add olive oil, salt, and black pepper and toss to combine.
3. Place vegetables in an even layer in the air fryer basket. Air-fry vegetables until roasted, about 20 minutes, stirring halfway through cooking time.

Nutritional Information

- Calories: 69
- Fat: 4g
- Carbs: 7g
- Protein: 3g

Henry Wilson

8. Desserts

Nutella-Banana Sandwiches

Preparation Time: 10 minutes

Yield: 2 Servings

Ingredients

- ½ cup butter, softened
- 4 slices white bread
- ¼ cup chocolate hazelnut spread (Nutella)
- 1 banana

Directions

1. Pre-heat the air fryer to 370°F.
2. Spread the softened butter on one side of all the slices of bread and place the slices, buttered side down on the counter. Spread the chocolate hazelnut spread on the other side of the bread slices. Cut the banana in half and then slice each half into three slices lengthwise. Place the banana slices on two slices of bread and top with the remaining slices of bread to make two sandwiches. Cut the sandwiches in half (triangles or rectangles) – this will help them all fit in the air fryer at once. Transfer the sandwiches to the air fryer.
3. Air-fry at 370°F for 5 minutes. Flip the sandwiches over and air-fry for another 2 to 3 minutes, or until the top bread slices are nicely browned. Pour yourself a glass of milk or a midnight nightcap while the sandwiches cool slightly and enjoy!!

Nutritional Information

- Calories: 237
- Fat: 14g
- Carbs: 26g
- Protein: 3g

Henry Wilson

Molten Lava Cake

Preparation Time: 10 minutes

Yield: 4 Servings

Ingredients

- 1.5 TBS Self Rising Flour
- 2 Eggs
- 3.5 TBS Baker's Sugar (Not Powdered)

- 3.5 OZ Unsalted Butter
- 3.5 OZ Dark Chocolate (Pieces or Chopped)

Directions

1. Preheat your Air Fryer to 375F
2. Grease and flour 4 standard oven safe ramekins.
3. Melt dark chocolate and butter in a microwave safe bowl on level 7 for 3 minutes, stirring throughout. Remove from microwave and stir until even consistency.
4. Whisk/Beat the eggs and sugar until pale and frothy.
5. Pour melted chocolate mixture into egg mixture. Stir in flour. Use a spatula to combine everything evenly.
6. Fill the ramekins about 3/4 full with cake mixture and bake in preheated air fryer at 375F for 10 minutes.
7. Remove from the air fryer and allow to cool in ramekin for 2 minutes. Carefully turn ramekins upside down onto serving plate, tapping the bottom with a butter knife to loosen edges. Cake should release from the ramekin with a little effort and center should appear dark/gooey. Enjoy warm a-la-mode or with a raspberry drizzle.

Nutritional Information

- Calories: 540
- Fat: 14g
- Carbs: 53g
- Protein: 4g

Shortbread Heart Cookies

Preparation Time: 10 minutes

Yield: 2 Servings

Ingredients

- 250 g Plain Flour
- 75 g Caster Sugar
- 175 g Butter
- 1 Tsp Vanilla Essence
- Chocolate Buttons

Directions

1. Preheat the air fryer to 180c.
2. In a mixing bowl place all your ingredients apart from your chocolate and rub the fat into the other ingredients.
3. It will soon rub into each other to create a nice soft dough.
4. When it is a big dough ball roll it out and cut it into heart shapes with your cutter.
5. Place it into the air fryer on top of a baking sheet with a little gap in between each one. Cook for 10 minutes on 180c.
6. Open the air fryer and place the chocolate buttons into the top of the half baked dough.
7. Cook for a further 10 minutes on 160c and serve with hot chocolate and marshmallows.

Nutritional Information

- Calories: 190
- Fat: 11g
- Carbs: 21g
- Protein: 2g

Henry Wilson

Vegan Beignets

Preparation Time: 20 minutes

Yield: 4 Servings

Ingredients

FOR THE POWDERED BAKING BLEND:

- 1 cup Whole Earth Sweetener Baking Blend
- 1 teaspoon organic corn starch

FOR THE PROOFING:

- 1 cup full-fat coconut milk from a can
- 3 tablespoons powdered baking blend
- 1 1/2 teaspoons active baking yeast

FOR THE DOUGH:

- 2 tablespoons melted coconut oil
- 2 tablespoons drained water from a can of chickpeas
- 2 teaspoons vanilla
- 3 cups unbleached white flour, with a little extra to sprinkle on the cutting board for later

Directions

1. Add the Whole Earth Baking Blend and corn starch to your blender and blend until powdery smooth. The cornstarch will keep it from clumping so you can store it if you don't use it all in the recipe.
2. Heat the coconut milk until it's warm but cool enough that you can stick your finger in it without burning yourself. If it's too hot, you will kill the yeast. Add it to your mixer with the sugar and yeast. Let sit 10 minutes, until the yeast begins to foam.
3. Using the paddle attachment, mix in the coconut oil, aquafaba, and vanilla. Then add the flour a cup at a time.
4. Once the flour is mixed in and the dough is coming away from the sides of the mixer, change to your dough hook if you have one. (If you don't, keep using the paddle.)
5. Knead the dough in your mixer for about 3 minutes. The dough will be wetter than if you were making a loaf of bread, but you should be able to scrape out the dough and form a ball without it staying on your hands.
6. Place dough in a mixing bowl and cover with a clean dish towel and let rise for 1 hour.
7. Sprinkle some flour over a large cutting board and pat out the dough into a rectangle that's about ⅓ inch thick. Cut into 24 squares and let it proof for 30 minutes before you cook them.

8. Preheat your air fryer to 390 degrees. Depending on the size of your air fryer you can put 3 to 6 beignets in at a time.
9. Cook for 3 minutes on one side. Flip them, then cook another 2 minutes. Since air fryers vary, you may need to cook yours another minute or two for them to get golden brown.
10. Sprinkle liberally with the powdered baking blend you made in the beginning and enjoy!
11. Continue cooking in batches until they are all cooked.
12. Preheat your oven to 350 degrees. Place the beignets on a baking sheet covered with parchment paper.
13. Bake for about 15 minutes or until golden brown. Sprinkle liberally with the powdered baking blend you made in the beginning and enjoy!

Nutritional Information

- Calories: 102
- Fat: 3g
- Carbs: 15g
- Protein: 3g

Apple Pie

Preparation Time: 30 minutes

Yield: 4 Servings

Ingredients

- 1 Pillsbury Refrigerator pie crust
- Baking spray
- 1 large apple, chopped

- 2 teaspoons lemon juice
- 1 tablespoon ground cinnamon
- 2 tablespoon sugar
- ½ teaspoon vanilla extract
- 1 tablespoon butter
- 1 beaten egg
- 1 tablespoon raw sugar

Directions

1. Defrost pre made pie crust according to package directions.
2. Pre-heat the Airfryer on the highest degree while you are preparing the pie.
3. Using the smaller baking tin, cut 1 crust about an ⅛ of an inch larger than the tin and a second one a little smaller than the baking tin. You may need to roll the crust a tiny bit with a rolling pin to stretch the pie crust. Set the smaller one aside.
4. Spray the baking tin with the baking spray and place the larger cut crust into the baking pan. Set aside.
5. In a small bowl, place the chopped apple, lemon juice, cinnamon, sugar, and vanilla extract. Mix to combine.
6. Pour the apples into the baking pan with the pie crust.
7. Top apples with pieces of butter.
8. Place the second pie crust over the top of the apples and pinch edge. Make a few slits in the top of the dough.
9. Spread beaten egg over the top of the crust and sprinkle raw sugar over the top of the egg mixture.
10. Place pie in Air Fryer basket.
11. Set the timer for 30 minutes at 320 Degrees

Nutritional Information

- Calories: 243
- Fat: 10g
- Carbs: 36g
- Protein: 5g

Zebra Butter Cake

Preparation Time: 30 minutes

Yield: 4 Servings

Ingredients

- 115g butter
- 2 eggs
- 100g castor sugar
- 100g self raising flour, sifted
- 30ml milk
- 1tsp vanilla extract
- 1 tbsp of cocoa powder

Directions

1. Preheat airfryer at 160C. Line the 6" baking tin base and grease the side of the tin
2. Beat butter and sugar in mixer till fluffy
3. Add eggs one at a time then add vanilla extract and milk. Mix well in mixer
4. Add sifted flour and mix till incorporated
5. Scoop half batter out and set aside
6. Add cocoa powder to the batter in mixer and mix well
7. Scoop 2 tablespoons of the plain batter on center of baking tin. Then scoop 2 tablespoons of chocolate batter on the centre of the plain batter in the baking tin. Keep scooping by alternating both batters until finish. After every scoop of batter into the tin, try to tap the tin to let batter spread out.
8. Place baking tin in airfryer and bake at 160C for 30 minutes or until the skewer emerges cleanly.

Nutritional Information

- Calories: 380
- Fat: 17g
- Carbs: 55g
- Protein: 2g

Thai-Style Fried Bananas

Preparation Time: 40 minutes

Yield: 4 Servings

Ingredients

- 4 Ripe Bananas
- 2 tablespoons All Purpose Flour
- 2 tablespoons Rice flour
- 2 tablespoons Corn flour
- 2 tablespoons Desiccated Coconut
- 1 pinch Salt
- 1/2 teaspoon Baking powder
- 1/2 teaspoon Cardamom Powder, (optional)
- Cooking oil, to drizzle
- 1/4 cup Rice flour, for coating

- Sesame seeds, for coating

Directions

1. To begin making the Fried Bananas, get all the ingredients together and keep them handy.
2. We will begin by making the batter for the fried bananas. Into a large bowl, add in the all purpose flour, rice flour, corn flour, baking powder, salt, coconut and stir to combine well. Next add in little water at a time to make a thick and almost smooth batter. The batter should be such that it can coat the back of a spoon.
3. Keep the rice flour and sesame seeds ready.
4. If you are using mini bananas (almost a large finger size), then slice it lengthwise into half. If you are using a large banana, then cut it into half, then slice it half lengthwise. Keep it aside.
5. Next grease a 8 x 8 inch foil or a butter paper with oil and dust it with flour. This is so that when we air fry the batter dipped bananas, they don't stick to the foil or the paper.
6. Fit the foil or the butter paper pinching the ends so as to leave a little gap for air circulation.
7. Dip banana slices into the wet batter, then roll the wet batter coated banana slices into the dry rice flour and then onto the sesame seeds. I like adding sesame seeds to the top as it adds a crunchiness to the air fried bananas.
8. Place the batter dipped bananas into the greased foil or butter paper. Air fry the bananas at 200C for about 10 to 15 minutes, flipping half way through so it gets fried evenly all around.
9. Once ready, serve the Thai Crispy Fried Bananas as a tea time snack or even as a dessert served along with vanilla ice cream.

Henry Wilson

Nutritional Information

- Calories: 378
- Fat: 22g
- Carbs: 44g
- Protein: 5g

Air Fryer Cinnamon Rolls

Preparation Time: 20 minutes

Yield: 8 Servings

Ingredients

- 1 pound frozen bread dough, thawed
- ¼ cup butter, melted and cooled
- ¾ cup brown sugar
- 1½ tablespoons ground cinnamon

Cream Cheese Glaze:

- 4 ounces cream cheese, softened
- 2 tablespoons butter, softened
- 1¼ cups powdered sugar

- ½ teaspoon vanilla

Directions

1. Let the bread dough come to room temperature on the counter. On a lightly floured surface roll the dough into a 13-inch by 11-inch rectangle. Position the rectangle so the 13-inch side is facing you. Brush the melted butter all over the dough, leaving a 1-inch border uncovered along the edge farthest away from you.
2. Combine the brown sugar and cinnamon in a small bowl. Sprinkle the mixture evenly over the buttered dough, keeping the 1-inch border uncovered. Roll the dough into a log starting with the edge closest to you. Roll the dough tightly, making sure to roll evenly and push out any air pockets. When you get to the uncovered edge of the dough, press the dough onto the roll to seal it together.
3. Cut the log into 8 pieces, slicing slowly with a sawing motion so you don't flatten the dough. Turn the slices on their sides and cover with a clean kitchen towel. Let the rolls sit in the warmest part of your kitchen for 1½ to 2 hours to rise.
4. To make the glaze, place the cream cheese and butter in a microwave-safe bowl. Soften the mixture in the microwave for 30 seconds at a time until it is easy to stir. Gradually add the powdered sugar and stir to combine. Add the vanilla extract and whisk until smooth. Set aside.
5. When the rolls have risen, pre-heat the air fryer to 350°F.
6. Transfer 4 of the rolls to the air fryer basket. Air-fry for 5 minutes. Turn the rolls over and air-fry for another 4 minutes. Repeat with the remaining 4 rolls.
7. Let the rolls cool for a couple of minutes before glazing. Spread large dollops of cream cheese glaze on top of the warm cinnamon rolls, allowing some of the glaze to drip down the side of the rolls. Serve warm and enjoy!

Nutritional Information

- Calories: 143
- Fat: 8g
- Carbs: 17g
- Protein: 1g

Henry Wilson

Air Fryer Cranberry Pecan Muffins

Preparation Time: 20 minutes

Yield: 8 Servings

Ingredients

- 1/4 cup cashew milk (or use any dairy or non-dairy milk you prefer)
- 2 large eggs

- 1/2 tsp. vanilla extract
- 1 1/2 cups Almond Flour
- 1/4 cup Monkfruit (or use your preferred sweetener)
- 1 tsp. baking powder
- 1/4 tsp. cinnamon
- 1/8 tsp. salt
- 1/2 cup fresh cranberries
- 1/4 cup chopped pecans

Directions

1. Add to blender jar the milk, eggs and vanilla extract and blend 20-30 seconds.
2. Add in the almond flour, sugar, baking powder, cinnamon and salt – blend another 30-45 seconds until well blended.
3. Removed the blender jar from the base and stir in the 1/2 of the fresh cranberries and the pecans. Add the mixture to silicone muffin cups. Top each of the muffins with remainder of fresh cranberries.
4. Place the muffins into the air fryer basket and bake on 325 for 12-15 minutes – or until toothpick comes out clean.
5. Remove from air fryer and cool on wire rack.
6. Drizzle with a maple glaze if desired. I also drizzled melted white chocolate over some of the muffins.

Nutritional Information

- Calories: 143
- Fat: 8g
- Carbs: 17g
- Protein: 1g

Henry Wilson

Air Fryer Homemade Pop Tarts

Preparation Time: 20 minutes

Yield: 6 Servings

Ingredients

- 2 refrigerated pie crusts
- 1 tsp cornstarch

- 1/3 cup low-sugar strawberry preserve
- 1/2 cup plain, non-fat vanilla Greek yogurt
- 1 oz reduced-fat Philadelphia cream cheese
- 1 tsp sugar sprinkles
- 1 tsp stevia
- olive oil or coconut oil spray

Directions

1. Lay the pie crust on a flat working surface. I used a bamboo cutting board.
2. Using a knife or pizza cutter, cut the 2 pie crusts into 6 rectangles (3 from each pie crust). Each should be fairly long in length as you will fold it over to close the pop tart.
3. Add the preserve and cornstarch to a bowl and mix well.
4. Add a tablespoon of the preserve to the crust. Place the preserve in the upper area of the crust.
5. Fold each over to close the pop tarts.
6. Using a fork, make imprints in each of the pop tarts, to create vertical and horizontal lines along the edges.
7. Place the pop tarts in the Air Fryer. Spray with oil. I prefer to use olive oil.
8. Cook on 375 degrees for 10 minutes. You may want to check on the Pop Tarts around 8 minutes to ensure they aren't too crisp for your liking.
9. Combine the Greek yogurt, cream cheese, and stevia in a bowl to create the frosting.
10. Allow the Pop Tarts to cool before removing them from the Air Fryer. This is important. If you do not allow them to cool, they may break.
11. Remove the pop tarts from the Air Fryer. Top each with the frosting. Sprinkle sugar sprinkles throughout.

Nutritional Information

- Calories: 274
- Fat: 14g
- Carbs: 32g
- Protein: 3g

Conclusion

We hope you enjoyed the book on "Air Fryer Recipes".

Air fryers are easy to operate and can be used by just about anyone. The fryer is designed to cook food at a faster pace, thereby saving time, while keeping the flavor of the dish.

Printed in Poland
by Amazon Fulfillment
Poland Sp. z o.o., Wrocław